CULTURE**SHOCK!**

A Survival Guide to Customs and Etiquette

KOREA

Sonja Vegdahl
Ben Seunghwa Hur

GRAPHIC ARTS®
BOOKS

mc **Marshall Cavendish**
Editions

Photo Credits:
All photos from Korea National Tourism Corporation and Sonja Vegdahl ▪
Cover photo: R Ian Lloyd

All illustrations by TRIGG

First published in 1988
Copyright © 2005 Marshall Cavendish International (Asia) Private Limited

This edition published in 2005 by:

Marshall Cavendish Editions
An imprint of Marshall Cavendish International (Asia) Pte Ltd
1 New Industrial Road, Singapore 536196
Tel: (65) 6213 9300, fax: (65) 6285 4871.
Email: te@sg.marshallcavendish.com
Online bookstore: www.marshallcavendish.com/genref

and

Graphic Arts Center Publishing Company
P.O. Box 10306, Portland, Oregon 97296-0306
United States of America
Tel: (503) 226 2402
Website: www.gacpc.com

Please contact Graphic Arts Center Publishing Company for the Library of
Congress catalogue number

ISBN 981-261-128-2 (Asia & Rest of World)
ISBN 1-55868-936-2 (USA & Canada)
ISBN 0-462-00812-6 (Europe)

Printed in Singapore by Times Graphics Pte Ltd

ABOUT THE SERIES

Culture shock is a state of disorientation that can come over anyone who has been thrust into unknown surroundings, away from one's comfort zone. *CultureShock!* is a series of trusted and reputed guides which has, for decades, been helping expatriates and long-term visitors to cushion the impact of culture shock whenever they move to a new country.

Written by people who have lived in the country and experienced culture shock themselves, the authors share all the information necessary for anyone to cope with these feelings of disorientation more effectively. The guides are written in a style that is easy to read and covers a range of topics that will arm readers with enough advice, hints and tips to make their lives as normal as possible again.

Each book is structured in the same manner. It begins with the first impressions that visitors will have of that city or country. To understand a culture, one must first understand the people—where they came from, who they are, the values and traditions they live by, as well as their customs and etiquette. This is covered in the first half of the book

Then on with the practical aspects—how to settle in with the greatest of ease. Authors walk readers through how to find accommodation, get the utilities and telecommunications up and running, enrol the children in school and keep in the pink of health. But that's not all. Once the essentials are out of the way, venture out and try the food, enjoy more of the culture and travel to other areas. Then be immersed in the language of the country before discovering more about the business side of things.

To round off, snippets of basic information are offered before readers are 'tested' on customs and etiquette of the country. Useful words and phrases, a comprehensive resource guide and list of books for further research are also included for easy reference.

CONTENTS

FOREWORD

Many of your experiences in Korea will be fascinating, pleasurable and thought-provoking. Others will be confusing, infuriating and embarrassing. The expatriate who has adapted to living in Korea feels fortunate to live in this dynamic but small, mountainous country; the newcomer often feels the frustrations of culture shock.

The majority of people who have made Korea their home for any period of time, find that it is a land with many things to love: the closeness with nature reflected in the architecture; the physical beauty of this mountainous country; the warmth and friendliness of the people; the evidence of history and tradition blending comfortably with modern ways and more convenient structures. Many aspects of Korea are naturally attractive.

But even the most pleasant country can become a miserable place to live in when one does not know how to get cash out of an ATM, buy a bottle of shampoo or catch a taxi. It is not so much that things are different, for most newcomers are able to accept different values, customs and patterns of behaviour in other people, and eventually learn to go about their lives in a different way. The most difficult aspect of being transplanted into a new culture is that it seems impossible to comprehend. There seem to be so many dichotomies that cannot be understood from western perceptions. Then, as soon as you think you are about to understand this ancient culture, something happens to contradict what you thought you had figured out.

We hope in this book to help you understand Korea, so that most of your encounters with this rich eastern culture will be satisfying. In learning, you will not only be preparing yourself for an easier adjustment to a colourful and unique culture, but you will be expanding your concept of how people of different nationalities think, feel, act and communicate.

A word or two of caution before you read this book. The first is that we write from our own perspective. Our experiences and those of people we met in Korea may not ring true to others. The second is that Korea is changing at a rapid pace. Korea is a different country than when we wrote the first edition of this book in 1988. Things are noticeably different today than they were even five years ago. This edition reflects the significant changes that have occurred in the customs and lifestyles of Korean people and, to the best of our ability, represents Korea in 2005. Each region, family and individual changes in its own way, at its own speed. What is described in this book are general attitudes, patterns of behaviour and customs that many Koreans exhibit today. Certainly, there will be Koreans who do not fit these descriptions.

Having said that, we can also say that there are few people, Korean or non-Korean, who can claim to be familiar with every bit of information in this book. In the course of our research, particularly this recent update, we were constantly surprised at how little we ourselves knew about a culture we had lived in for many years. And even more at how little many Koreans of this generation knew about their own customs.

We hope you will find pleasure in reading our book, just as we enjoyed writing it.

Sonja Vegdahl
Ben Seunghwa Hur
USA, 2005

ACKNOWLEDGEMENTS

Writing this book would have been impossible without the help of many people. We would like to thank our parents who instilled in us an interest in and acceptance of people from other cultures. Throughout the writing of this book, they gave the kind of encouragement and support only they could have given.

We would also like to thank our students, Korean and non-Korean, who gave us general and specific insights into many of the topics covered in the book. Many of you do not know how much you stimulated us, as we were 'teaching' you.

We would like to thank individuals from a few organisations that offered generous assistance for this edition: numerous Fulbright English Teachers working in Korea, members of the Canadian Women's Club, members of International Lutheran Church in Seoul and members of the Working Women's Network in Korea. The various perspectives each of you generously shared with us added greatly to our understanding of the various experiences of people living in Korea today.

To many others too numerous to mention, both Koreans and expatriates, who spent untold hours carefully reading what we have written, giving helpful advice on the content, our sincere thanks. Untold errors have been avoided through your careful scrutiny. Your enthusiasm about this book kept us going during the times the task seemed beyond us. You can be sure your questions and experiences will benefit others. As we would say in Korean, 'Kamsa-hamnida'.

To our sons,
Anders and Erik

MAP OF THE REPUBLIC OF KOREA

CHINA

NORTH
KOREA

KOREA
BAY

E A S T

S E A

●SEOUL

**REPUBLIC
OF KOREA**

YELLOW SEA

KOREA STRAIT

JAPAN

JEJU STRAIT

JEJU-DO

FIRST IMPRESSIONS

CHAPTER 1

"A journey of a thousand miles begins
with one single step"
—A Korean Proverb

UNLIKE BETTER-KNOWN JAPAN AND CHINA, few westerners know much about Korea, despite its 5000 year old history. Old photos of The Korean War may be the only image many have of this peninsular country. Sports fans may have seen footage of Korea during the 1988 Seoul Olympics or the 2002 soccer World Cup that Korea and Japan co-hosted. People familiar with international foods may have been introduced to kimchi, the Korean national dish. Only when someone has a reason to learn about Korea, due to relocation orders or an extended business trip or travel do many begin to explore this East Asian country.

Some coming to Korea may have had the impression that Korea is a developing country and are surprised how advanced it is. As the 11th largest economy in the world, Korea has fully joined the developed countries of the world. Some expatriates will find access to services they did not have in their own countries.

Most people coming to Korea fly into Inchon International Airport which opened in 2001. When Seoul Airport was unable to handle the growing numbers of international travelers the airport was built on land reclaimed from the ocean. This airport is spacious, convenient and easy to navigate with signs in English, Chinese, and, of course, Korean. People at the airport speak varying amounts of these foreign languages so without much trouble one should be able to accomplish the things one needs to do at an airport: go through immigration, get one's luggage, go through customs, exchange money and find transportation to one's final destination. Seoul is a bit over an hour from Inchon by limousine bus or taxi, both of which are easy to take. Transportation connections to other parts of the country are also conveniently accessed just outside the airport.

Moving away from the airport one initially will see hotels, parking and restaurants, as one would see outside any airport. Newly planted trees and immature landscape along the expansive expressway gives way to mostly rural land: small hills compact farms, greenhouses and clusters of houses. The closer one gets to Seoul the denser the buildings and traffic become. Many foreigners find the multi-storey cement apartment buildings aesthetically unpleasing. Others find these apartment buildings familiar as they are similar to those in other highly populated cities of the world.

Korea used to be called the 'land of the morning calm' but now Koreans have adopted the term 'dynamic Korea' which is a better description of what metropolitan life is like in major Korean cities, which is where most expatriates live. The twenty storey cement apartment complexes, some with more than 25 buildings, are tightly packed in among the buildings needed in any modern city: restaurants, grocery shops, petrol stations, office buildings, internet café's, coffee shops, hotels and schools. Some are struck by how many neon-lit red crosses, symbolizing Christian churches, there are. Expatriates coming to Seoul will also notice many familiar names: Baskin-Robbins, Pizza Hut, KFC, Starbucks, Outback Steakhouse, Burger King, and Olive Garden are among the many international chains that are ubiquitous.

Arts and Crafts

The Korean National Tourism Organization has an area at Inchon Airport where people who have time on their hands can do Korean crafts, free of charge. Recently, unpainted clay Korean dolls were given to anyone with the time and inclination to paint a doll. Tables were set up with a selection of paints and young women clad in traditional hanbok (Korean dress) were available to answer questions in English, Chinese and Korean and to help with the painting. Upon finishing the project, the dolls were glazed and then wrapped in bubble wrap and put in a pretty box. The whole task took about an hour. The projects, all related to Korean culture, change regularly.

As one of the densest countries in the world, one cannot help but notice how crowded Korean cities are. It is not an exaggeration to say that there are thousands of enormous apartment buildings, unlike anything most people have seen. People are walking and driving everywhere, even quite early in the morning and quite late into the night. Though Seoul now has roads as modern and well-maintained as any international city, the traffic congestion is apparent and the driving style is troubling to most expatriates experiencing Korea for the first time, particularly during the extended rush hour periods.

Many expatriates coming to Korea are struck by how nicely dressed Koreans are. Others notice that, though Koreans all have black hair, there is much diversity in terms of facial structure and body size and type. In recent years, it has been noticeable that there are very few young children in public. One might think this is because children don't go out much in public, but in fact, it is primarily because Korea now has one of the lowest birthrates in the world. Their population control programme, which begun in the 1960's and was held up as a model programme, became too successful and now the government has a campaign to encourage couples to have more children. A bonus is paid to families having a third child. Like the governments of Japan, Singapore and many European countries where the birth rate is below replacement, the government of Korea is concerned that there will not be enough workers and taxpayers to support the rapidly expanding number of seniors.

In Seoul, one might be surprised that though you may look quite different from everyone around you, few people stare at foreigners or even seem to notice how different you may look. The Seoul City Hall estimates that 1 per cent of the city residents are foreign so Seoul residents have grown quite used to seeing foreigners moving among them.

Outside metropolitan areas, the landscape, naturally, is quite different. Expatriates travelling to rural areas or small cities are surprised by how much open space there is, given the density of Korea. Visitors to Korea are uniformly struck by how beautiful the country is, as motorways wind along streams, past patchworks of rice fields, and beside rugged but small mountains densely packed with trees and other vegetation. In the winter, the landscape may be covered with snow; in the autumn with brightly coloured deciduous leaves and in spring and summer by a brilliant shade of green. Surprisingly, clusters of enormous cement apartment buildings pop up in the midst of bucolic farmlands.

In rural areas, western-looking people clearly stand out and may be stared at. People who are fair-haired, blue-eyed, tall or obese and children draw the most attention. People in rural areas welcome the opportunity to meet foreigners but, at the same time, may be shy or uncomfortable around people who look different. Koreans one may encounter outside metropolitan areas have less opportunity to practise their English. On the other hand,

The Latest Craze

People returning to Korea after ten years absence and first time visitors to Korea are likely to notice a new trend: dogs have become quite popular. One can see small dogs peeking out from purses or blankets in unexpected places, such as on the underground or in the arms of someone walking down the street. To meet the needs of this rapidly growing obsession, pet stores have sprung up, selling everything a city dog owner could need: clothes, food, toys and shampoo. One may also notice pet beauty shops that cut, style, and dye the tresses of these beloved family members.

many expatriates experiencing rural life find people to be especially warm and friendly, eager to help foreigners adjust to life in their country.

Expatriates from western countries are frequently struck with how friendly Korean people are to them. If you look foreign and pull out a map, it is more likely than not that someone will ask if you need help. Though Koreans are not uniformly pleased with the policies of various western countries, Koreans are generally warm and welcoming to individual foreigners and will go to surprising lengths to help them.

LAND, HISTORY AND RELIGION

CHAPTER 2

'When whales fight, it is the shrimp
whose back gets broken.'
—A Korean Proverb

GEOGRAPHY

Korea's history is greatly influenced by its geographic location; surrounded by larger countries not always at peace with one another or with Korea. The Korean peninsula is bounded by China, the former USSR and Japan. North and South Korea are artificially divided by a 2,000-kilometre demilitarised zone, at roughly the 38th parallel. The total land area of South Korea is 221,370 sq km (85,471.4 sq miles, about the size of New Zealand). It is mountainous, broken up by narrow valleys, abundant small streams, long rivers and flat, fertile plains. It is divided into nine provinces and seven metropolitan areas. Approximately half the population lives in those seven metropolitan regions.

Korea is a 'tilted' country, with the higher regions in the northeast, and the lower in the southwest. The mountain range on the eastern coast is rugged, at places appearing higher than in reality. Few peaks on the peninsula exceed 1,200 m (3,937 ft). These rocky eastern mountains meet the ocean abruptly, making the eastern coast a very scenic one. The western and southern coasts are extremely irregular, with some 3400 islands, the most famous being Cheju Island. Much of Korea's cultivated land (20 per cent of the total area) is in the south. Minerals, on the other hand, are more abundant in North Korea.

The population of the Republic of Korea, in the south, is about 48 million, making it one of the third most densely populated countries in the world, denser than both India and Japan. North Korea is far less crowded, with a population about half as large as that of the Republic of Korea. Much of Korea's history, up to the present day, has been influenced by its geography. The location of the Korean peninsula has made Korea particularly valuable for more powerful countries.

HISTORY
Beginnings

According to Korean legend, a heavenly king, Hwanin, sent his son, Hwanung, to earth. There he married a bear-turned-woman. They had a son, Tan-gun, the founder of the Korean race. Koreans celebrate Tan-gun's birthday as a national holiday, on 3 October, called Kae Chun Chul, literally 'sky opening day'.

Archaeologists believe that tribes from the Altai mountains began migrating to Manchuria and Siberia around 4000 BC. Some of them continued on to what is now the Korean peninsula, and settled there. These tribes eventually formed three kingdoms, which were first united in AD 668 under the Shilla dynasty. The Koreans share distinct physical characteristics, the same culture and one language, all of which have helped them retain their own identity, despite thousands of years of foreign invasions and several prolonged periods of non-Korean rule. Koreans today are deservedly proud of their old, enduring and unique culture, and of the race that they call their own.

The Three Kingdoms (c. 37 BC–AD 668)

Chinese records date the founding of Korea at 1122 BC. There are few records of Korean history until the time of the Three Kingdoms. The Koguryo kingdom was in the north, the first to emerge as a major power, and the first also to adopt Buddhism. The Paekche kingdom in the southwest developed next, and became known for its artistic creations. Finally, the Shilla kingdom came into being, emphasising military strength. These three kingdoms co-existed until 668, when the Shilla kingdom conquered the other two and unified the Korean peninsula.

The Unified Shilla Period (668–935)

The Shilla period ushered in great artistic accomplishments. Buddhism became the state religion, and even peasants subscribed to a simple form of Buddhism. The capital was located in Kyongju, a famous tourist spot today. As time passed, the economic disparity between the rulers and the ruled increased. Some of the leaders became corrupt, and internal power struggles among the leaders finally brought about the downfall of the government.

The Koryo Dynasty (935–1392)

The new dynasty, which lasted 400 years, was founded by Wang Kun. The Confucian system of government examinations for choosing civil servants by merit was adopted. The well-educated civil servants could censure royal decisions. Exquisite Koryo celadons were created during this period, and literature flourished. In 1238, the Mongols, who had taken control of China, swept over the Korean peninsula, destroying many Buddhist temples and works of art.

One of the many reminders of Korea's history, this pagoda is part of Kyongbokkung Palace, built in 1392, which is located in downtown Seoul.

Internal problems also existed. Buddhist and Confucian scholars, who had co-existed peacefully until this time, came into conflict. Advocates of Confucianism, which had now reached Koryo, criticised the lavish spending on temples and opposed the custom of monks leaving their families, as this conflicted with the strong Confucian emphasis on filial piety. Yet another problem were the Japanese invasions. Previously on a small scale, by the mid-thirteenth century Japan had become an organised military power.

When the Mings took the Chinese throne from the Mongols, they disposed of the Koryo king who had supported the Mongols against them. This gave General Yi Song-gye an opportunity to seize the Koryo throne.

The Yi Dynasty (1392–1910)

The first Yi king moved the capital to Seoul, then called Hanyang (*Han* for river, *Yang* for the life-giving force). Castles were constructed there, and walls were built around the city.

To combat the corruption of the former Koryo government, and to give his own government legitimacy, the new ruler's first priority was to establish Confucianism. The anti-Buddhist movement of the late Koryo period continued, targeting Buddhism as the source of corruption and moral laxity. Strict Confucian rules, such as the separation of men and women, were put into practice, especially among the *yangban* (upper) class.

King Sejong

King Sejong ruled from 1418 to 1450 and is considered one of the greatest rulers in Korean history. His accomplishments were many and varied. Advances were made in the study of history, political studies, medicine and Confucian studies. Sundials, water clocks and rain gauges were invented. Agricultural information was compiled and distributed to the peasants.

King Sejong is best known for the creation of *hangul*, the Korean alphabet *(see Chapter 8, Communicating)*. Until then, only scholars were able to read, since mastering the Chinese characters used took many years of concentrated study.

Foreign Invasion

In the late 1500s, the Japanese navy invaded the southern coast of Korea repeatedly with increasing power. The Koreans fought bravely, but had little chance against the numerically superior Japanese. Admiral Yi Sun Shin is known for his strong turtle boats which defeated the Japanese many times, but he, too, was finally killed in battle.

The fighting stopped when the Japanese emperor, Hideyoshi, died in 1598, but many towns along the Korean coast had been badly damaged. (At that time the Japanese captured some skilled makers of ceramics, who later helped develop the craft in Japan.)

The Hermit Kingdom

While Korea always maintained relations with China and Japan, it became increasingly wary of opening its doors to the West. It was afraid Western ideas would undermine the strong influence of Confucianism. Missionaries to Korea, while managing to convert some people, were sometimes killed. Missions from other countries were rejected and Korea's isolationist policies branded it the 'Hermit Kingdom'.

The Japanese Annexation (1909–1945)

While Korea was trying hard to keep out foreign influences, Russia, China and Japan were engaged in a power struggle to occupy Mongolia and Korea. After Japan had defeated China in 1895 and Russia in 1905, it forced Korea to accept the 'Protectorate Treaty' which regulated Japan's control over Korea's administrative and foreign relations functions. This treaty had the support of the United States and Britain. Although Korean uprisings to protest against this move were numerous and brave, Japan's military power was able to suppress the resistance, and eventually Japan annexed Korea. Japan controlled all aspects of Korean life —communication, transport, fisheries, timber, mining and land ownership. Children were educated in the Japanese language, and Koreans were forced to give up their names and adopt Japanese ones. Studying Korean history was illegal. Many Koreans were taken to Japan to work and serve in the Japanese army.

The Beginning Of The Republic Of Korea

When Japan surrendered at the end of World War II, the United States and the USSR, both leery of the increasing power of the other in East Asia, agreed that the Korean land south of the 38th parallel would be temporarily administered by the United States. The Koreans had no say in this division. The area north of the 38th parallel was to be administered by the USSR. But later, the two Korean regions, and the two superpowers overseeing them, were unable to reach an agreement on a unification formula. In 1948, Syngman Rhee was elected president of the south and Kim Il-Sung took power in the north.

The Korean War (1950–53)

In 1949, the United States withdrew its troops from Korea. The USSR also removed its troops, but left a well-trained and well-equipped North Korean military force. In June 1950, North Korea invaded its southern counterpart. Seoul was taken in three days, and within a month, the whole peninsula was controlled by the North except for the town of Pusan on the south coast.

The United States and other United Nations members sent reinforcements and pushed back the North Korean troops. But communist Chinese troops arrived to aid the North, forcing the UN troops to retreat. The UN forces gathered up strength, and again pushed the Northern troops back to roughly the area of the 38th parallel.

In July 1951, armistice talks began between the two halves, but a treaty was only signed two years later. It was only a temporary ceasefire agreement, and subsequent attempts for a more permanent agreement have all failed. The demilitarised zone remains unchanged.

The Korean War left the country in ruins. Thousands of families experienced the death of a family member.

Thousands of orphans were left. Families were separated by the division of North and South. The economy and agricultural base suffered near total destruction.

Postwar Developments In South Korea

Syngman Rhee served as president of South Korea until he was forced to resign in April 1960. Chang Myon was elected prime minister in June 1960. Chang's government was unable to deal with the massive problems facing Korea, and a bloodless military coup overthrew it in May 1961.

Park Chung Hee, then a general, took over the government. Later, he resigned from the military and was elected as a civilian president. During the Third Republic, which lasted 17 years, unparalleled economic development was achieved.

In October 1979, Park was assassinated. Choi Kyu-hah was president for a short spell. He declared martial law but massive demonstrations continued. In December 1979, General Chun Doo Hwan took control of the government. He was indirectly elected in March 1981 for a single 7-year term.

In December 1987, the first direct presidential election was held. While charges of fraud were made, Rho Tae Woo, a former military academy classmate of Chun Doo Hwan, became the seventh president of the Republic of Korea. The Republic of Korea and North Korea were both admitted to the United Nations in October 1991, thus realising a long-held dream for many Koreans.

In 1992, Kim Young Sam defeated his long-term opposition party rival, Kim Dae Jung, in a presidential election. President Kim Young Sam began his administration by attacking bribery and corruption in the government. This led to the discovery that former presidents, Chun Do Hwan and Rho Tae Woo, had both illegally garnered significant wealth during their presidencies. Chun was also convicted for his pivotal role and later cover-up in what is termed the 'Kwangju Massacre'. Later, Kim Young Sam and his family were also found to be involved in illegal, wealth-generating activities.

In an interesting turnaround, Kim Dae Jung, long considered too radical for most Koreans, was elected president in 1997. He took office just as the Asian economic crisis was beginning to have a serious and severe impact throughout Korea. The Asian financial crisis of 1997–1999 exposed longstanding weaknesses in South Korea's development model, including high debt/equity ratios, massive foreign borrowing and an undisciplined financial sector. Growth plunged to a negative 6.6 per cent in 1998, then strongly recovered to 10.8 per cent in 1999 and 9.2 per cent in 2000. The International Monetary Fund set up a strict plan to pull Korea out of serious financial problems. Koreans responded to the crisis with their usual hard work, sacrifice and perseverance. Most families experienced turmoil during this period, as husbands lost jobs and their status in the family and members were forced to take jobs they normally would not have done.

In 2002, Korea was the proud co-host of the 2002 FIFA World Cup. The event marked the first time that the World Cup had been held in Asia. The 64 tournament soccer games were divided equally between Korea and nearby Japan. Koreans used this opportunity to showcase their beautiful country and to demonstrate their warm hospitality. The feeling of national pride was evident throughout the country, as people wore red in support of their own talented football team.

President Roh Moo Hyun, who took office in February 2003, ran on the Millennium Democratic Party, the party of former president Kim Dae Jung. President Roh has long been a champion of the poor and was a human rights lawyer, which resulted in his imprisonment at an earlier time in his life. This election was close and President Roh could not have been elected without the strong support of the younger generation in Korea. In his presidential campaign, Roh made it clear that he would continue former president Kim Dae Jung's reunification policy (a policy that resulted in Kim being awarded the Novel Peace Prize in 2000). Like every administration before his, Roh's administration has also been marked by scandal. His five-year presidential term ends in 2008.

Since the dangers of potential nuclear aggression from North Korea is frequently discussed outside of Korea, people unfamiliar with South Korean life may imagine people there are living in constant fear. In fact, South Koreans and expatriates living in Korea feel quite safe. North Korean angry rhetoric is primarily directed at the United States, particularly after the North Korea was labelled an 'Axis of Evil' country by the president of the United States. President Roh has made overtures towards North Korea and a limited number of exchanges have taken place between divided families (some living in the north, others in the south) and businesses.

RELIGION

Like many other aspects of Korean life, religion is a mixture of beliefs introduced by people from other countries, and modified to fit Koreans. The earliest religion was a form of animism, paying tribute to the ten thousand spirits of nature. Buddhism entered Korea during the period of the Three Kingdoms (37 BC–AD 668). Confucianism, which served the function of religion, predominated during the Yi dynasty. Christianity was first introduced during the Japanese invasions in 1592, but did not gain a foothold in Korea until much later About half of the Korean population actively practice religion. Among this group, Christianity and Buddhism comprise Korea's two dominant religions. A smaller number of people practice Shamanism (traditional spirit worship) and Chondogyo ('Heavenly Way'), a traditional religion.

Buddhism

Buddhism probably has the largest following of any organised religion in Korea. According to some records, it was introduced, via China, to the northernmost kingdom, Koguryo, in AD 372, then spread to the other two kingdoms, becoming especially prominent during the Unified Shilla period (AD 668–935). At that time, many Buddhist temples were built throughout Korea, and monks were revered.

Buddhism continued to flourish during the Koryo dynasty (AD 935–1392). A treasured cultural relic of the Koryo dynasty

Buddhist monks pray to enter the nirvana circle around the Tabot'ap Pagoda at the courtyard of Pulguksa Temple. This pagoda is considered a masterpiece of stone sculpture surviving from the Shilla period.

and a significant landmark in the history of Buddhism are the 81,258 wooden printing plates of the ancient Buddhist scripture, the Tripitoka, carved between 1237 and 1252. (The first movable metal type was developed in Korea in 1377, some 200 years before Gutenberg.) After prominence in the Koryo dynasty, Buddhism lost the status it enjoyed when the Yi dynasty came into power in 1392. Buddhism was blamed for much social corruption and Buddhist monks were driven out of Seoul.

During the Japanese annexation, Buddhism became visible again as the Japanese promoted similarities between Korea and Japan. But only in recent years has Buddhism been able to regain some of its popularity. There are now more than 7 million avowed Buddhists, and perhaps twice that many practise the faith in some way or other. There are about 25,000 clergy of both sexes, and monks are seen throughout Korea in their grey robes and pointed straw hats. Koreans of all faiths appreciate the 7244 accredited temples scattered in picturesque locations throughout the country.

As Buddhism has been a presence for thousands of years, even non-Buddhist Koreans have absorbed some of its subtle aspects. For instance, because of their belief in Buddhist karma, Koreans have developed a fatalistic, accepting approach to their problems, as well as great patience in dealing with difficulties that they believe to be inevitable.

Buddhist temples are common tourist destinations for Koreans and expatriates alike. A serene temple nestled against a mountain, surrounded by the fresh blooms of spring, flaming colours of autumn, or snow-topped hillsides, is a quick cure for the stress one feels from fast-paced city life. Buddhist temples are found throughout the country, in remote areas as well as in cities. Generally, a number of buildings are located inside the stone wall which surrounds the temple area. Visitors are free to look around at will-taking photographs and talking quietly are not discouraged. The building which holds a statue of Buddha usually has several steps and an open sliding door at the top of the stairs. If one desires to go inside, shoes must be left in the area near the sliding doors. Buddhists then enter the room, bow once or several times towards the Buddha statue, and meditate for a while, sometimes putting incense on the altar. Others may enter this room as well, taking care to be quiet.

Christianity

Korea's first contact with Christianity was probably during the Japanese Hideyoshi invasions of 1592–1598, when a Roman Catholic priest accompanied the Japanese General Konishi Yukinaga, a Catholic convert. The priest didn't convert any Koreans, however.

In 1777, during the reign of King Chongjo, a young scholar, Yi Sung Hun, went to Beijing where he was introduced to Christianity by Jesuit missionaries, and was baptised. Upon his return, he converted many Koreans, including members of a prominent family, and the first Christian church was founded. Korean Catholics today take great pride in the fact that Christianity was introduced to the country by the laity, and not by missionaries.

At the end of the 18th century, there were about 4000 Christians, but practising Christianity in a strongly Confucian country was rather difficult. Christians often refused to perform ancestral ceremonies, which did not make them popular with the Confucian government. Persecution of the Catholic missionary movement drove it underground.

Protestantism made its first major inroad in 1884, when Dr Horace Allen came to Korea as a physician for foreign diplomatic officers. Later, as the royal family physician, he went on to found the first Western-style hospital. The Protestants had the advantage of entering Korea more than a century after the Catholics, learning from their failure. Moreover, they worked within the government system, focusing on providing health care and education.

Koreans embrace many things with enthusiasm so it is not surprising that Korean Christians take their beliefs and the teachings of their church quite seriously. Some foreigners in Korea, as well as native Koreans, find Christian proselytising, by friends and strangers alike, to be troublesome. One is likely to be exposed to more such incidents in Korea than in one's home country.

During the Japanese occupation, both Protestantism and Catholicism gained popularity amongst Koreans. The Christian ideals of humanity, social mobility, equality and democracy were particularly attractive at that time.

After many Christians escaped from North Korea to the south during the Korean War, South Korea's Christian churches grew remarkably. Today there are about 11 million Christians in Korea, roughly 25 per cent of the total population, the second highest percentage of any East Asian country after the Philippines.

Places of Worship

There are a wide variety of churches, synagogues and mosques with services available in several western languages. Information about these is given in English-language newspapers every Saturday. Joining a familiar place of worship is an excellent way to ease oneself into an unfamiliar culture. Most international places of worship are particularly sensitive to the needs of expatriates, and their members provide support for one another.

As with Buddhism, Christianity has left its mark on all Koreans. The Christians introduced the concept of education for women and equality of the sexes. Christian leaders in Korea today are actively vocal about social problems, and many are highly respected.

Shamanism

Advocates of Buddhism, Confucianism and Christianity in Korea made some very strong attempts to eradicate shamanism, but none succeeded. Besides serving a religious function in the lives of Koreans, shamanism provides entertainment, not to mention psychological and social benefits.

So entrenched is the belief in spirits, that aspects of shamanism have been incorporated into the other religions. Observe, for example, that most Buddhist houses in Korea have a spirit house. Some Christian rituals, such as praying for long periods, were perhaps more readily accepted by Koreans because of the similarity of these acts to shamanistic traditions.

Doubtless in this same spirit of sharing, aspects of other religions have also been incorporated into shamanism. Some shamanistic spirits took on the image of Buddha when Buddhism spread across Korea. And when Confucianism stressed the need for women to bear sons, it suddenly became general knowledge that the Mountain Spirit had the ability to produce sons.

Perhaps shamanism exists today in Korea because of its ability to co-exist with the other religions. Shamanistic ceremonies are held when international companies open new multi-storied offices in Seoul. When western medicine and traditional Korean medicine both fail to cure an illness, a shaman is summoned to perform a kut or exorcism *(see page 22),* in case evil spirits are the culprits.

Many Koreans participate in shamanistic rituals. For some, they are a source of entertainment; for some others they are a mere formality. For the rest, the spirits exist and must be appeased to prevent misfortune.

According to shamanism, spirits exist in every part of nature. Every river, mountain, animal and home has a spirit. Everyone who dies has one, that may or may not move on to another world. These spirits are not inherently good or bad, but if treated badly, they bring about misfortune, including sickness, natural disaster and family discord. When worshipped or summoned, however, they help

Two shamen totem poles stand guard against evil spirits.

prevent problems and ensure good luck. Koreans are careful to summon the right spirit. For example, the Dragon King assists by providing bountiful rain, but has no power to cure an illness.

Mudangs

The *mudang* or Korean shaman, who is always a woman, has the special ability to communicate with spirits and is the go-between of the spirit world. There are records of *mudangs* from as early as the Shilla period, when, even then, they were women. *Mudangs* have played an important role in Korea's history as they were close to the rulers, advising on state affairs. During the Yi dynasty, despite government damping down of shamanistic practices, *mudangs* were still employed by the royal family. In fact, they were among the few women allowed to have contact with men.

Mudangs are thought to be 'called' by the spirits to serve that function. A woman, single or married, may have had a psychotic episode where she loses contact with people. The only way she can escape such episodes is by becoming a mudang. There are families of hereditary *mudangs* who earn a living visiting villages to perform annual or biannual ceremonies, the villagers' insurance of adequate rain, health and general prosperity.

With her special ability, one would have imagined that the mudang was revered, but this is not the case. On the contrary, she is considered to belong to one of the lowest social classes in Korea, even by those who consult her. Koreans would be ashamed to own up to having a *mudang* in the family.

Kuts

A *kut* is a shamanistic ceremony during which a *mudang* makes spiritual contact. Ceremonies range from the very simple (one *mudang*, a client and a few friends) to the dramatic (several *mudangs,* costumes, props and a large audience). Simple *kuts* last a few hours, large ones run to several days and great expense.

The purpose is to resolve a problem, usually serious, such as an illness or a downturn in business. A *kut* is especially important when a family member has died prematurely-unmarried or childless-for the spirits of such people are reluctant to move on to the next world. They remain tied to earth, creating problems for their living relatives. It is imperative, therefore, to persuade them, via the *mudang*, to travel smoothly to the next world.

At a larger *kut*, the *mudang* will wear various costumes symbolising the spirit she is trying to attract. A drummer beats out a rhythm, the mudang sings, chants and dances, at first slowly, then teasingly and violently, to attract a particular spirit. When the spirit arrives, he speaks through the mudang: a deceased relative may want to express some last thoughts; a living relative may wish to convey something; a dissatisfied spirit may make demands.

An important part of the *kut* is the drama. The bright colours, fans, knives and lanterns set the stage for the advent of spirits. It is lively entertainment for the audience who may even join in the dancing.

The *mudang*'s performance must be convincing. She becomes not only a spirit medium, but an actress, dancer, magician, comedienne and musician. When speaking for the general spirit, she may balance on two razor-sharp knives with bare feet. During the *kut*, she may hold out her fan, asking the audience to donate coins to the greedy spirit. She may walk across a 'bridge' made only of paper, held high in the air by two assistants. The *mudang* may rip long white cloth with her body, symbolising the final separation between the deceased and the living.

FORTUNE TELLING

Many Koreans today seek the advice of a fortune teller at particular times: mothers consult one before their children marry, to determine the compatibility of the new couple; parents confirm the suitability of a newborn baby's name; families require advice over the appropriateness of a burial site for a family member. Fortune tellers are especially busy before a university entrance examination and at the beginning of the year, when people need advice in planning the year's activities. It is not uncommon for businessmen

Ko Bong-seok, inside Kyongbokkung Palace in Seoul, an old hall where Confucian ceremonies of the Yi dynasty were held.

to consult fortune tellers before making important business decisions. Christians generally do not seek out advice from fortune tellers.

A Korean's fortune depends primarily on the year, month, day and time of birth, collectively known as *saju*. Twelve animals represent different years, months, days and times, and the combination of these animals is thought to determine one's future.

In Korea, visiting a psychologist is considered a sign of mental weakness, but it is perfectly acceptable to visit a fortune teller. In many ways, they serve the function of mental health professionals. They are supportive and sympathetic towards their clients, and can reduce the guilt and responsibility suffered for unfortunate incidents. A deserted wife may be told, for example, that her present circumstances are her 'destiny', and beyond her control.

CONFUCIANISM

Confucianism is a philosophy or code of conduct, not really a religion but Confucianism has shaped Korean society in a way that nothing else has. In fact, many believe that Korea was influenced more by Confucianism than Confucius' native country, China. Understanding Confucianism can help expatriates in Korea make sense of many aspects of Korean culture.

Confucius, or K'ung Ch'iu, was a teacher and philosopher born in China in 551 BC. He believed leaders should be highly educated, that government should be in the hands of the most capable people rather than controlled by nobles, that everyone in society had a role, and if that role was carried out correctly, society would be just and good.

Confucius' teachings about the social structure of society and his system of education were first introduced to Korea during the Three Kingdoms (37 BC–AD 668). But they gained popularity only during the Yi dynasty (AD 1392–1910), when Buddhism was blamed for social corruption and Confucianism was upheld as a way to restore social order.

Confucian Ideals for Social Conduct

In Korea, Confucianism became a strict set of rules for social conduct, the effects of which can clearly be seen today.

Confucianism stressed the harmony of social relationships. Emotions were to be suppressed, and everyone was to follow the correct social order, so as not to disrupt the flow of society. The five most important relationships were specified, and the proper attitude governing these relationships was delineated.

Of these five, only the last one was a horizontal or equal relationship. The position of a person became as important as, if not more important than, who the person was. Korean

Types of Confucian Relationships

- Between Father and Son
  (characterised by affection and filial piety)
- Between Ruler and Subjects
  (characterised by righteousness and loyalty)
- Between husband and wife
  (characterised by distinction in position)
- Between Elder and Younger
  (characterised by respect)
- Between Friends
  (characterised by trust and loyalty)

social relationships today are still, by and large, vertical. Each person knows his position in relation to other people, and acts accordingly.

FAMILY

According to Confucian philosophy, the family is the basis of society. The leader of the country is the 'father' of his people and is ultimately responsible for their welfare. They, in turn, owe him their respect. Within a family unit, the father is responsible for the care of his family. If a family member violated a law, the father is accountable, as he should have raised that person to respect the law.

GOVERNMENT

Selflessness and moral purity are necessary Confucian qualities for responsible, ethical leaders. People believed they had a right to expect such leaders, and also the right, moreover, to monitor their actions. An annual government examination, covering a diverse range of subjects, was used to select leaders.

During the Yi dynasty in Korea, only people of the high yangban class were eligible to take this examination. Though Korea has not often had such noble leaders, most Koreans today still judge government leaders at all levels by these high Confucian moral standards. A corrupt government officer, once discovered, is expected to be quickly relieved of his post. Similarly, a leader is held accountable for transgression committed by those under him.

EDUCATION

Confucianism's stress on the importance of education has influenced all Asian countries. Even second and third generation Asians in western countries, on a whole, tend to perform better than their non-Asian counterparts.

The value of education is similarly deeply impressed upon Koreans. Education and working hard is seen as the only path to success, as well as a valuable pursuit in and of itself. Koreans today hold a special reverence for teachers and relationships between teachers and students can be lifelong.

The Confucian emphasis on education can be seen today, as vast numbers of students compete for places in the top universities of Korea.

ROLES OF MEN AND WOMEN

While few question the positive effects in Korea of Confucian respect for elders and education, many criticise the effect Confucianism has had on the lives of Korean women.

During the Unified Shilla period (668–935), women enjoyed nearly equal legal status with men. But in the latter part of the Koryo dynasty (935–1392) and even more in the Yi dynasty that followed, Confucianism dictated inequality for women. Boys and girls were permanently separated after the age of five. Sons of the high or yangban class received an education in Confucian classics, and later were eligible to compete for the government examination. Girls remained with their mothers, learning housecraft until they were married, and controlled by their mothers-in-law as soon as they were married.

The husband or parents-in-law of a transgressor of one of these evils had the right to turn her out. She was, moreover, forbidden to return to her parents' home. No matter what their husbands did, however, women could not divorce them.

The Seven Evils

Traditionally, a woman was forbidden from committing any of *chilgo chiak* (seven evils):

- Disobeying her in-laws
- Bearing no son
- Committing adultery
- Jealousy
- Carrying a hereditary disease
- Excessive chatter
- Larceny

During the Yi dynasty, women were not supposed to be seen by non-family members. They remained confined at home. In the evening, a bell would ring, warning men off the streets so that women could go out briefly. Some were less fortunate: one older Korean woman recalls being thrilled when her family escaped to Pusan during the Korean War, as it was her first glimpse beyond the walls of her home.

While Korean women today have much more control over their lives, their gender still restricts their choices. Boy babies are generally preferred to girls, because boys remain part of the family, whereas girls are only temporary members who leave their parents when they marry. However, today it is not unusual to meet young people who prefer a daughter. Until recently, women's legal rights were not equal to men. Now fathers are not automatically given custody of their children when a divorce occurs and women can be the legal head of household, eliminating the requirement that a grown woman have a father or son sign off on legal documents.

THE KOREAN PEOPLE

CHAPTER 3

'As for clothes, the newer the better.
As for friends, the older the better.'
—A Korean Proverb

ONE OF THE BEST PARTS OF BEING IN KOREA for most expatriates is the experience of knowing people from a country quite unlike their own. Coming to understand how people think, act and see the world so differently from oneself is also likely to be a source of difficulty during one's time in Korea. This chapter begins by introducing the reader to characteristics and values that Koreans commonly share. The importance of the family to Koreans and the Korean life cycle, from birth to old age, will be described. The chapter will end with a discussion of the importance of regional differences in Korean's perceptions of one another.

It is difficult to attribute traits to a nation's people, as there are often almost as many exceptions to any rule as there are conformers. But newcomers to Korea and long-term residents alike do notice some particular 'Korean' characteristics and these are worthy of elaboration.

CHARACTERISTICS AND VALUES COMMON TO KOREAN PEOPLE
National Pride
Koreans are universally and rightly proud of being Korean. They value their accomplishments, history, their language and their rich and enduring cultural traditions. Korean pride gives people a strong, positive identity and explains many aspects of their interactions with foreigners. While Koreans recognize that they are relatively unknown to people in

much of the world, they are clearly pleased when expatriates show an interest and knowledge in Korea. While Koreans regularly discuss and criticise aspects of their own society, until they know and trust an expatriate, they will be quite uncomfortable sharing and hearing negative comments about Korea. Some expatriates experience this as defensiveness.

Family

Family occupies an important role in the lives of all Koreans. Koreans rejoice in their family members' accomplishments and share in one another's' disappointments. They worry nearly as much about a family member's troubles as about their own. Though family structure and roles are changing, Koreans still have many obligations towards one another and share a close intimacy. *(Family will be discussed in more detail later in this chapter)*.

Interpersonal Relationships

Not unlike the closeness, loyalty and responsibility one feels towards one's family, is the web of relationships that all Koreans value and nourish. To westerners, the energy and time one devotes to these relationships can seem excessive. Most Koreans have monthly gatherings with different groups of friends; some even meet monthly with the alumni of their kindergarten. Besides being fun, these relationships are useful in managing the challenges of one's life: securing jobs for oneself or other family members, borrowing money and finding out about educational or business opportunities. These responsibilities to friends can be burdensome to Koreans but neglecting them is unimaginable.

Emotional Expression

Within their Confucian framework, emotions must be discreetly controlled in public. But hiding behind the sometimes-stoic Korean façade is a multitude of emotions. And when Koreans are among friends and close family members, feelings are shared freely. When old friends see one another their faces readily light up and their happiness is visible to anyone nearby. Likewise, negative emotions may be expressed with passion. It is not unheard of for national legislators to strike one another when their anger takes over. Koreans have been called the Irish of the East and expatriates living in Korea generally agree. People with higher status or rank show negative feelings more freely than those of lower rank. Koreans are especially sensitive to their own and other people's feelings, and such emotions play a big role in everyday behaviour. Positive emotions are strongly felt and expressed as warmth, loyalty and compassion.

Kindness Towards Those One Knows

Many expatriates are struck with the kindness bestowed upon them by Koreans. People will go to great lengths to help out someone they care about. Expatriates have had Korean friends devote a whole day to helping them find a particular household item. Other expatriates have been awed by the generosity showered on them by their co-workers and neighbours: invitations to go on outings to cultural sites, lavish meals prepared in their honour and thoughtful gifts brought back from trips abroad. Treating people related to them by blood, work or friendship with thoughtfulness and care is an ordinary occurrence in Korea. Such hospitality is rarely conferred on those one is not connected to though it is not unusual for foreigners to be treated with care by Koreans whom they don't know.

Simple Pleasures

Individual Koreans relish things such as cold noodles on a hot day or seeing a particular friend they have missed. Being able to satisfy those cravings is important to Koreans. Friends and family understand such passions and, when possible, help one another get what they want. They also pay attention to the strong likes of those they love and will make great efforts to get the desired object; for example, buying a friend a favourite food or seeking out just that favourite colour for a scarf or tie. Individual tastes are valued and appreciated.

Hard Work

Few foreigners live in Korea long without noticing the extreme efforts Koreans will put forth to accomplish something important. This begins in childhood, when children are required to study late into the night, to increase their chances of entering a top university. Koreans generally believe that if they work hard enough, they can achieve almost anything. Their hard work no doubt is a key component to their business, academic and artistic success both in their own country and abroad.

Humility

Koreans value humility and do not appreciate people who boast about their accomplishments. Most Koreans minimise their own achievements, saying, for example, that 'my business is doing okay' when, in fact, it is thriving. Sometimes expatriates mistakenly take comments Koreans make about themselves at face value and, as a result, misunderstand. One is unlikely to find out about achievements from an individual him or herself; however, his or her friends are likely to inform you. Since your Korean friend is unlikely to talk about her or his accomplishments to others, when you are introducing your friend it is appropriate for you to tell the other person about your friend's accomplishments. Your friend, however, is likely to smile and deny that she or he has done anything special. Knowing that westerners commonly share their success, some Koreans will refrain from being so modest when conversing with foreigners.

Sense Of Humour

Although Koreans are diligent, controlled and patient, they also possess a striking sense of humour. This characteristic has enabled them to persevere under difficult circumstances and also makes life more fun. Korean humour is evident in folk art, masked dances, puppet shows and even shamanistic exorcisms. Almost any gathering of Koreans seems to include at least one person with a special ability to make others laugh. Unfortunately for the foreigner, Korean wit does not always retain its humour when translated. Still, expatriates and Koreans who become friends generally find humorous situations that transcend cultures.

Kibun

To understand Korean interpersonal relationships, behaviour and thought is to know the concept of *kibun*. Like other culture-laden words, there is no exact English equivalent.

Kibun relates to mood, current feeling and state of mind. To hurt someone's *kibun* is to hurt his pride, to cause loss of dignity and to bring about loss of face.

Korean interpersonal relationships operate on the principle of harmony. Maintaining a peaceful, comfortable atmosphere is more important than attaining immediate goals or telling the absolute truth. Koreans believe that to accomplish something while causing unhappiness or discomfort to individuals is to accomplish nothing at all. If relationships are not kept harmonious, it is difficult, if not impossible, to work towards any goal. All cultures value how their members feel emotionally, but few cultures value this as much as Koreans do. To Koreans, to put greater emphasis on efficiency, honesty or some higher form of moral integrity, is to be cold and unfeeling.

Kibun enters into every aspect of Korean life. Knowing how to judge the state of other people's *kibun*, how to avoid hurting it, and keeping your own kibun in a satisfactory state are important skills.

Those who ignore the significance of *kibun* will find many unnecessary obstacles in their paths. If you need something done, for example, but can see that the *kibun* of the person required to do it is not in a good state, it would be foolish to make the request. (The means by which one judges another's *kibun* is called *nunchi*. This is discussed below.)

To foreigners, Koreans may seem overly sensitive and emotional, and their kibun seems to be hurt too easily. For example, an older Korean's *kibun* may be damaged when his subordinate does not show proper respect, that is, by not bowing soon enough, not using honorific words, not contacting the superior within an appropriate period of time, or worse, handing something to him with the left hand. Most of these rules of etiquette are well known to Koreans, and while they are often difficult or cumbersome to remember, they should be heeded to avoid hurting *kibun*.

Sometimes, even for Koreans, the rules are not clear and one can inadvertently damage someone's *kibun*. If you do not know the person's position in relation to yourself, and treat him as an inferior, his *kibun* may be hurt, and he may not wish to continue a relationship with you. Or, in ignorance of the fact, you may say something derogatory about his home town. You may even mistakenly believe an older classmate to be in the same 'class' and call him by name, rather than addressing him as hyung (older brother).

When interacting socially with Koreans, it is essential to bear in mind the importance of *kibun*. As a foreigner, you will be forgiven some offences. But the more value you place on kibun as opposed to accomplishing material goals, the more respected you will be, and the better your relations with Koreans will be.

Bad news-a negative financial report or an employee's error, for example-is generally brought to an office at the end of the day, to give the recipient time to recover before the next day. And people are almost always fired without any notice, for who can continue working when their kibun has been so badly damaged? Giving a less expensive gift than the receiver would deem appropriate can also injure *kibun*.

As Korea is a hierarchical society, this sensitivity is most important with regard to people of a higher status. A superior often does not consider the feelings of those of lower status. But then inferiors have less face to lose! If a husband rebukes his wife in public, she is not nearly as humiliated, her *kibun* is not as damaged as her husband's would be in the reverse situation.

Nunchi

Closely tied to *kibun* is another Korean concept, *nunchi,* which literally means 'eye measure'. It is the ability to assess another person's *kibun*, but it is done not only by the eye.

In a society where behaving so as not to disturb social harmony is critical, being able to judge another person's state of mind is essential. Good nunchi ability puts a person one step ahead of everyone else. He will know when to ask his boss for favour, when to take or yield the right of way in traffic, and when to tell bad news and cause the least damage.

Nunchi is a kind of antenna one has to sense another's feelings or state of mind. Some of this is done by watching body language, heeding the tone of voice and what is said. In Korea, where *kibun* is so important, many people have developed a kind of sixth sense with which to assess it.

Of course, this kind of judgment takes place everywhere in the world, as when a child learns the best time and person to ask for an ice cream or treat. But whereas westerners are more likely to state their moods, or at least reveal their states of mind, Koreans have been taught to control their emotions, and to disguise their true feelings. To discern the mood of a Korean requires much *nunchi*.

Some Koreans complain about the indirectness with which they are required to express their feelings. They would sometimes prefer to say exactly how they feel, and often wish others would do the same, thus negating the need for such a sensitive nunchi. But tradition dies hard in this Confucian-oriented society.

Remember, too, that the temperature gauges of feelings in Korean and western societies are different. Thus, an angry outburst may be taken as an expression of greater dissatisfaction in Korea than in a western country. If you receive a phone call bearing bad news, and appear sad after it, your Korean friend will probably treat you with extra care and sensitivity, afraid to upset you further. If you complain to your subordinate about being behind on a project, she may misinterpret this to mean that you are generally dissatisfied with her work.

Know the Signs

It is impossible for people from different cultures to consistently read one another's verbal and non-verbal messages accurately. Being aware of the sensitive way your own mood is being judged by others, particularly by people of lower status, may help you understand their behaviour.

The Family

The Korean family has undergone rapid change in the last generation. Most young people choose their own spouse and couples no longer live with the husband's parents. Divorce, which was formerly rare, is as common in Korea as in other developed countries. Still, understanding Koreans is understanding the critical role that family plays in the lives of Koreans.

Following Confucian dictates, the traditional Korean family was based on the male family line. An extremely important document, the family register, includes the names of a Korean's paternal ancestors for over 500 years. The continuity of this bloodline is critical and, until recently, possible only by having sons. Family lines existing for many generations tragically ended when a male offspring does not produce a male child. In 2005, the national government adopted a plan to grant parents the right to choose to put their children on their father's family registry or the mother's family registry. Few couples are expected to choose their mother's family line but having this as an option would have been unthinkable even a decade ago. Traditionally, only a male could be the head of the family. This has resulted in some unusual situations such as a single or divorced mother needing her five-year-old son's signature on legal documents. This too has changed, giving women the right to head a household.

Respect for Parents and Ancestors

Koreans have a long tradition of valuing the knowledge and experience of their parents and grandparents. While Korean parents today do not make decisions for their grown children, parents and grandparents have a stronger influence on those decisions than their western counterparts. For example, Korean young people look to their parents for guidance on what to major in or which job to take. Ancestral ceremonies are held in honour of deceased parents several times a year. They are performed for the three previous generations (parents, grandparents and great-grandparents). Ancestral ceremonies are performed only for one's paternal ancestors. Wives honour their husband's ancestors.

While young people today do not show the high level of respect accorded to their parents and grandparents in days past, they still show more respect that young people from most western countries. As young people have eased up on the formal respect that they show their parents, they have increased the comfort they feel around their older relatives. Consequently, many young people today are more comfortable relaxing with

Three old men enjoying one another's company on a warm spring day.

their parents as they do not have the constraints that high respect entailed.

Extended Family

Nuclear family living arrangements are increasingly common and though the Korean family is undergoing significant changes, the extended family continues to hold an important role in people's lives.

For Koreans, the conception of family consists of grandparents, their sons, the sons' wives and the sons' children. If a family is fortunate to have four living generations, all are included in the family. Members of this family unit are intimately tied to each other, and one member's affairs are every members' concern. Korean language distinguishes between relatives by their gender, the side of the family they are on (paternal or maternal) and, in the case of paternal relatives, their position in relationship to one's father. One's father's older brother is literally called 'big father' and the father's younger brother 'little father'.

Other relatives on the father's side, such as great-uncles, their wives, second cousins and so on are also considered part of the family. They are all on the same family registry and share a family name. These more extended relatives participate in weddings and hwangap (61st birthday) celebrations, but other contact with them is not too frequent, unless they have a particularly close relationship. Koreans have fewer responsibilities towards these more distant relatives.

The attachment to maternal relatives is also important, particularly between mothers and daughters, and between siblings. Emotional and financial support is found in these relationships. When a woman is pregnant, she often lives with her mother. After childbirth, it is common for the maternal grandmother to help care for the baby. While the child's paternal grandparents are legally tied to him, many young couples find that social relationships are easier when the maternal grandparents babysit.

Care For The Elderly

Conventionally, the first son and his wife are responsible for taking care of the parents when they retire. Now, with much smaller families, members do what needs to be done to help out their elderly parents. Like many western societies, most Korean elders prefer living on their own as long as possible or moving to a senior living community (called 'silver town') if they have adequate financial resources.

A generation ago, when a first son married, he and his bride lived with his parents. The daughter-in-law had an obligation to obey her mother-in-law, learn the ways of the family (including how they season their food), and care for the ageing parents until their deaths. The responsibilities of daughter-in-laws has lessened greatly in the past decade as the older and younger generations have more resources and want more independence. Nevertheless, the relationship between a daughter-in-law and her mother-in-law can be tense. There is much variation between families.

Male Roles

The husband/father is sometimes referred to as the 'outside person'. His greatest responsibility is providing the family income. Traditionally, he had a greater sense of duty towards his parents than to his wife or children, but this has changed as nuclear families have become the norm. Younger men are taking a greater role in their household, caring for children and even cooking and cleaning, something unthinkable a generation ago.

Female Roles

The wife/mother has historically been responsible for all 'inside' work. As the 'inside person', she devoted herself to raising her children and providing a comfortable home for her family. There is a compensating factor. Women generally manage the household finances. After giving his entire salary to his wife, a man receives an allowance from her.

Traditionally, the relationship between a Korean man and his wife was not a close friendship. Rather, as the old Confucian doctrine prescribes, it was characterised by a distinction of roles. Recently, however, Korean women are demanding a more active role in society, working outside their homes. Many women want to obtain professional employment rather than focusing their efforts inside the home. Some are choosing to delay or forgo marriage. Recognising the expense and energy required to raise a child, some are choosing not to have children. This too was unthinkable even ten years ago.

Korean Women

While expatriates may observe Korean women being subservient to their husbands, Korean women generally are surprisingly powerful in their families. Some high-positioned men are fearful of their wives and alter their behaviour to avoid her wrath. Women generally gain power as they get older and having children, particularly sons, enhances their status. Having control of the family finances adds to the wife's power. The deference a Korean wife shows her husband in public does not indicate that she is obedient or submissive at home.

AN OVERVIEW OF THE KOREAN LIFE CYCLE

Every province, family and individual approaches each stage of life a little differently. The most typical stages of life are described below, but great variations occur, particularly because Korea has changed from a traditional, agricultural society to a fully developed one. Traditional customs were meaningful and effective when large, extended families lived near each other and when hours in the field were flexible. Some of the customs are still meaningful and practical, and the young are eager to participate in them. Others are expensive, time-consuming and cumbersome, and are being replaced by different, perhaps more appropriate practices.

Pregnancy And Birth

Koreans traditionally believed that it was their foremost duty to produce children, particularly boys, for their ancestors. Besides being a filial duty, this has also served as an insurance policy for old age, as sons were, and still partly are, responsible for taking care of their elderly parents physically and financially. Since the mid 1990's the obligation and desire to have children has markedly change. Many Korean couples today believe that having children is a choice not an obligation. Couples delay having children, particularly in metropolitan areas, until their late twenties and even into their thirties. Korean media report that Korea has the lowest birth rate in the world and having only one child is quite common today. Some couples are even deciding not to have children.

Prenatal care is the norm in Korea and births occur in hospitals which meet international standards. After the birth, most often it is the grandmother who cares for her own daughter and grandchild after the grandchild's birth. Just as nutrition during pregnancy is important, so to is food after the birth. Seaweed soup, rich in iron and iodine, is served

Telling One's Age

Koreans determine one's age differently than people in western countries. When a baby is born, she or he is 'one'. In some ways this makes sense as the baby has been growing for nine months at birth. Then everyone's age advances a year at New Year's, not on the anniversary of their birth. So a child born December 1 is one year old at birth and on January 1 the child becomes two. The following January she becomes three. Consequently, Koreans born the same time as a westerner are two years older before the westerner's birthday and one year older after the westerner's birthday (since westerners change their age on their birthday). If one's exact age is important, it makes sense to clarify if someone is stating an age in the Korean system or in the western system.

to the new mother in large quantities after the birth. Then, each year on a person's birthday, many families commemorate the day by serving that same seaweed soup.

Keeping the mother warm after giving birth is also considered important. Drinking cold drinks (particularly with ice) is avoided and wearing many layers of clothes, even when the weather is warm, is observed. Women believe that exposed skin after giving birth will lead to arthritis later in life.

Naming The Baby

Names are believed to bring good or bad luck to the individual and family, so fortune tellers are often consulted on this matter. A Korean name, with few exceptions, consists of three syllables. The first is the family name. The next two are the personal name, that by which the parents call their child. Traditionally, these three syllables were Chinese words represented by Chinese characters. Recently some Koreans have adopted pure Korean names for their children.

Before a baby is born, two complete names (a girl's and a boy's) are selected, usually by the eldest male relative on the father's side. The baby's family name (surname) will be the same as his father's though couples will soon have the option of giving the child their mother's family name. (Women retain their own family names after marriage, so a man and his wife have different family names.)

In many families, the second or third name is the same among all male cousins of the same generation. For example, Kim Chul Soo, Kim Chul Min and Kim Chul Seung could be cousins, the family name (Kim) and the generational name (Chul) being the same. The next generation of male cousins would have the same third name, for example, Kim Young Ho, Kim Jun Ho and Kim Jae Ho. The third generation would go back to using the second name as the generational name.

The One-Hundred-Day Celebration

This celebration is a big party. The *paik il* party, as the one-hundred-day celebration is called, is held for the child who, more often than not, is upset about all the fuss and strangers. *Ddok* (rice cakes) are prepared, in addition to a big feast. Sometimes one party is held for the father's family, another for the mother's, and yet one more for the father's colleagues.

Guests bring a nice gift to a *paik il* party. This is sometimes a set of small silver chopsticks and a soup spoon. A baby-sized gold ring and baby clothes are other common gifts. Neighbours will know about the event when they receive a plate of rice cakes and other goodies. Then they will promptly buy and bring over a gift, often clothes or a set of the Korean soft cotton underwear.

A studio photograph is also taken to commemorate this day. Traditionally, a boy was photographed naked to show off his prized 'pepper'. Girls were fully clothed. Today babies of both genders are fully clothed in their one-hundred-day photograph.

After one hundred days, the baby is no longer seen as such a fragile human being, and may be taken outdoors. The period up to one hundred days, historically, was the most vulnerable time in a child's life, and therefore wisely treated with caution. Until that time, family and friends thought better of publicly celebrating a new life, when the child might be too weak to survive.

Congratulations!

If a Korean neighbour or friend is pregnant, congratulations are in order. The Korean greeting is '*Im shin ul chook ha hahm ni da*'.

In many western countries, a baby gift is given as soon as the baby is born. A few Koreans do this too, and you can if you like, but it is not necessary. If you hear about the one-hundred-day celebration, you could give something around that time. For an acquaintance, clothes would be the most appropriate gift. For a close friend, or someone you have daily contact with, a set of silver chopsticks and spoon is nice.

If you have the good fortune to be invited to the one-hundred-day celebration, dress as you would to any social gathering-in conservative party clothes. Bring your gift,

Three friends hang out together.

and be prepared to stay many hours. You will enjoy a delicious feast. The Korean greeting for 'Congratulations on your one-hundred-day celebration' is '*Paik il ul Chook ha Hahm ni da.*'

First Birthday

Three generations ago it was not uncommon for a child to die before his first birthday. Today, with excellent medical care, surviving the first year is the norm, but the first birthday called ddol is still one to celebrate. In fact, in Korea, only one other birthday is of equal significance, the *hwangap* (61st birthday).

The ddol has some similarities with the one-hundred-day celebration, but it is on a larger scale. More food is prepared, more people are invited and perhaps even more parties given. Besides the regular feast, and the ddok that is served on all festivals and holidays in Korea, another kind of rice cake is served, the moo jee gae *ddok* (rainbow), which looks more like a layered western cake in pink, green, brown and white. Being made of rice, however, it is heavier and chewier.

First Birthday Costume

The child is dressed in the traditional Korean costume, a *hanbok* (han means Korea, and bok, clothes). The brightly coloured outfit is often made of silk. The boy's outfit consists of baggy silk trousers, shirt, vest and jacket. He wears a black hat embossed with gold decoration. The girl's costume is a miniature hanbok, such as her mother wears: long skirt and short top with long, rounded sleeves. She, too, wears a special hat.

Photographs

These are rather prescribed. The young child, dressed in hanbok, sits behind a huge table filled with food for the feast. Rice cakes and various kinds of fruit (which are also a clear indicator of the time of year) are piled beautifully with all the other foods.

The background is usually a paneled screen, with richly embroidered birds, flowers and trees. Parents, grandparents and other siblings are included in some of the photographs-often all in *hanbok*.

Western Birthdays

If your child has a first birthday in Korea, you can celebrate it whichever way you choose. Koreans will understand that your customs are important to you just as their customs are to them. But if you want a good excuse to invite some Korean friends or business associates, this would be a good time.

Choosing The Future

Sometime during the day, the child takes part in an act believed to give a glimpse of his or her future success. Some money, a pen, a piece of thread and a book will be set before the child, and the child is allowed to grab the most attractive object. If money is picked, wealth is the child's destiny; the pen points to a future as a writer: the thread indicates long life: and the book may only be picked by a future scholar. Some parents place the child close to a particular object in an obvious bid to influence destiny!

Gifts

The traditional first birthday gift was a gold ring. This was a kind of insurance before the days of bank savings accounts. Several gold rings could always be cashed in if medical treatment was needed and the family had no money. Today other gifts, such as clothes and toys are common.

If you are invited to such a party, usually verbally a day in advance, or even on the day itself, drop everything and go. It is an honour to be able to celebrate this important occasion, and the food will be among the best you will eat in Korea. Dress as you would when you visit a Korean friend's home, and bring a gift: appropriate ones are a gold ring, clothes or a toy. The correct Korean greeting of congratulation on a child's first birthday is: 'Chot tol ul chook ha hahm ni da.'

Early Childhood

Korean children enjoy happy, carefree lives until the age of six. This is evident from the smiles on their faces and from the way strangers treat them in public. Children are seen as valuable, entertaining, adorable and worthy of all the good things in life.

Koreans place special importance on the mother-child relationship. In expressing her love, a good Korean mother sacrifices herself completely. She stays up late if her child wants to play, even though she has to prepare breakfast at dawn for her husband. She has remarkable patience, and tries hard to make this time a memory of joys for her child. Today, mothers are expected to provide experiences for their young children that will give them every advantage in school so that ultimately, they are able to attend a prestigious university. Various classes and lessons, such a music, sports and language, begin before kindergarten. As the child gets older, the lessons fill their lives before and after school and consume an important part of the family budget.

Role Of The Extended Family

While the mother's role is special, all relatives have an interest in and responsibility for the children in the family. Korean children usually grow up with many caring adults in their lives, and a strong sense of security and love. Younger fathers are playing a greater direct role in their children's lives than did fathers in the past. In the recent past, when three generations lived together, it was often the grandmother who looked after the child while the mother did the more difficult work of cooking, cleaning and washing. Today grandmothers have interests outside of home and may not be so willing to babysit though some are the primary caregivers if the child's mother works outside the home. Compared to western families, the boundaries around the nuclear family are more flexible in Korea. Children may spend weeks or even years living with extended family when their parents' work or school prevents them from caring for their child.

Love And Leniency For Young Children

Your Own Little Stars!

Your own children will be a star attraction every time they go out in Korea, especially if they are light complexioned and especially outside of major metropolitan areas. When you take your child to the zoo, he may look at the elephants, but everyone else will be looking at him.

People who visit a home where there are children often bring gifts for them. Even strangers will buy a treat for a child. Koreans love children, no matter whose they are. Sometime this adoration can create a problem. In restaurants, they may be given free rein, sometimes so much as to disturb other patrons. Koreans do not seem to mind. Sometimes expatriates in Korea feel that young Korean children are overindulged and undisciplined; however, if one realises how hard life will be once school begins, it is understandable that Korean parents want to make the early part of their child's life easy and enjoyable.

Koreans find children irresistible and freely touch them. Many foreign children appreciate this attention (which comes with lots of ice cream and sweets), but some may not. If it is a problem, you may limit your time in large public places. You can shield your child from unwanted touches. You can also explain that this is the Korean way of showing their kindness and interest. Most children eventually understand this, as they will understand (probably before you do) the kind things Koreans are saying to them.

School Days

In contrast to their carefree and uninhibited early childhood, Korean schoolchildren lead serious lives. Korean Confucian tradition considers education one of the most important things in life, both for its own sake and to better one's material and social position. During the Yi dynasty, a child from an unknown family could bring wealth and fame to his family and village by passing the government examination. This stress on education continues.

Korea has one of the highest literacy rates in the world. Primary school begins at age 6 and lasts 6 years. To ease the transition into school, the first two years of primary school follow a shorter and more flexible schedule. Going to school on Saturday is the norm. Classes are large, about 50 students per classroom.

Since entering a top university is fiercely competitive, most of a child's education is aimed at getting a high score for the university entrance examination. While children in Korean schools learn more in most subjects than their western counterparts, much of the emphasis is on rote learning. Expatriate English teachers are surprised, however, that when given an opportunity, Korean children are able to be creative and think independently. This, combined with their education in the arts makes them anything but robots.

Serious studying beings in elementary school and becomes more intense as the year progress. Elementary students sometimes have hours of homework every day as well as classes and lessons at institutes. Mothers are responsible for making sure that their children study. This is especially true during secondary school as the university entrance examination comes closer. Mothers may prepare and pack two lunches each school day, one to be eaten at lunch, the other at dinner. During that time, children usually stay at school, or at private study halls, until ten at night, and continue studying at home until after midnight. Koreans have a saying that if one sleeps more than four hours a night during secondary school, one will not be able to enter the university. While that is surely an exaggeration, the last two years of secondary school are one of the most difficult in one's life, both for the child and his or her mother. Koreans are concerned about the stress this exam places on their children but as much as everyone values a top university education and as hard as students are willing to work, they have not found a better system.

Expatriates living in Korea are puzzled why anyone would put their children through what is required for possible admittance into a prestigious university. In Korea, entering an esteemed university means more than recognition of the child's intelligence and, upon graduation, that he or she has had an excellent education. Top companies in Korea often limit their hiring to graduates of these top universities. Further, the relationship one makes in a prestigious universities will link one to people in high positions throughout society which will serve useful in getting future jobs, housing and business contacts. Additionally, one's choices for marriage are greatly enhanced when one has the highest educational credentials. The benefits accrued by graduating from a top Korean university are also extended to one's children and family. In short, every aspect of one's life will be greatly improved by entering a prestigious Korean university.

Having Fun

The strict education system allows children little time to socialise outside of school. Their whole life revolves around studying and competing for high positions in their class. Even so, just as everywhere else in the world, Korean children do find time for fun: with their classmates on crowded bus rides home, during school athletic festivals or the bi-annual school picnics, and with their families on Sundays, their one free day in the week. Video games and instant messaging are naturally popular in this technologically advanced nation. Children get a month-long vacation in the summer and another month's vacation in the winter. The school year begins in March and ends in February.

Divided Families

A troubling trend in recent years affecting thousands of Korean families are extended geographical separations, at times lasting more than a decade. Some of these separations begin when a father is working in a foreign country and the family decides it is best for the children to finish their education in that country even after the father is transferred back to Korea. Other families choose to have the mother and child or children live abroad, hoping to improve the child's educational opportunities as Korean children educated abroad have some additional options for entering top universities in Korea. Such children are also likely to be fluent in another language (usually English) and so could attend foreign universities more easily. While these arrangements might give children an educational advantage, it does not foster closeness between family members and it does result in loneliness and sometimes extra-marital relationships.

Fortunately, the structure of Korean classes provides a high degree of support for secondary school students. Unlike their western counterparts that have individual schedules, Korean students stay together as a class throughout the day and so become quite bonded to one another. These relationships formed in secondary school are likely to last a lifetime. The homeroom teacher takes great interest in each of his or her students becoming like a third parent. The sense of community, both within each class of students and the school as a whole, is quite strong. Students, faculty and administrators take pride in the accomplishments of any of their students.

University Life

After three years of intense study in secondary school preparing for the entrance examination, university life is, for many students, a time to relax and enjoy life. Foreigners teaching at a Korean university often find the lack of academic discipline surprising, having heard how much Koreans value education. University life is a short break between the pressures of secondary school and the stressful life of a worker and/or parent.

The university one attends is determined primarily by the score achieved in the entrance examination. Fortunate and few are the ones who enter one of the three top universities. After their freshman year, students apply for a major and it isn't always based on their interest. Job opportunities, the requirements for a particular major and the opinion of parents all factor into this decision.

University students spend a great deal of time on social and extra-curricular activities. Universities have a variety of clubs, from broadcasting and newspaper production to drama and traditional martial arts. They demand much of a student's time, and lasting relationships are formed there.

Most male and many female students enjoy drinking alcohol and learning how to socialise with others, a prerequisite to being an adult in Korean society. A variety of quite inexpensive alcoholic beverages are available, the rice wine *makoli* for example, so price is no barrier. Areas surrounding universities are filled with restaurants, drinking places, bookshops and other shops catering towards the young.

If you are a teacher, you will be respected, but you must also live up to your responsibility as a dedicated, humane person who is not overly critical of the host culture. As with other social interactions in Korea, you should remain very flexible, enduring sudden cancellation of classes, some 'sharing' of answers (not perceived to be 'cheating' in Korea), and misunderstandings. On the positive side, you will have a wonderful opportunity to learn about Korea at close hand and to develop close relationships with Koreans; you will also be accorded greater status and prestige than

If you are a student in Korea, you can expect the pace of studying to differ from that in your home country. You might follow the Korean example and include independently directed study in your academic plans. Remember that if Koreans appear less academically inclined than many students in western universities, at school they studied 12 hours daily for several years before reaching university level, and so they see this period of their lives as a time of relative freedom.

would be your due in a western academic setting.

Military Service

All men in good health are required to serve about two years in the Korean Military. Many young men do this in the middle of their university career so that they can enter university right from secondary school and, after military service, they can graduate and immediately enter the workforce. During military service, men have infrequent contact with their family and friends. They usually return to civilian life with marked maturity and a clearer sense of direction for their life.

Early Adulthood

Young adults generally live at home during university life (unless their university is far from home). Unlike their western counterparts, Korean young adults also usually live at home until marrying. This is partly because the cost of housing is quite high but most parents and young adults also like living together. Young adults enjoy eating their mother's food and appreciate having their laundry done but equally important, they like having time with their parents. Parents of adult children also enjoy being together as a family. Families separated because of work or study miss one another and look forward to the time they can live together again.

Marriage

Single people of marriageable age in Korea are often asked *'Un chae kook soo reul muk ul soo it seul ka yo?'* ('When will I have a chance to eat noodles?') Noodles are often eaten at wedding receptions, so this is an indirect inquiry into the person's marriage plans. It can also be interpreted as pressure to marry. In Korea an individual's marriage seems to be everybody's affair.

The joining of two families and two people in marriage is significant in a Korean's life. The only two other events of equal importance are the first and 60th birthdays. In the past 30 years, many of the traditional marriage customs have changed and new ones have been adopted.

Finding A Partner

Marriage partners may be chosen in one of two ways. Most young people find their own partners, effecting 'love marriages'. If one is not able to find a marriage partner on their own they may enlist the help others: introductions by friends and family, dating services or a match maker. Some dating service organisations host parties to introduce young people to one another. Like other countries, people can meet one another through Internet dating services.

In arranged marriages, young people want to get the best partner possible, considering things such as attractiveness, education, job and family background. Young Koreans are not required to marry anyone they do not want to marry.

Preparing For The Marriage

Once a marriage date has been set, often a month or two ahead, both families are very busy. As with other family matters, most of the burden falls on the females in the household. Besides choosing the wedding ceremony hall and arranging for the reception, they must prepare gifts for one another's families.

'If you have three daughters, the pillars of your house will fall down' is an old but partly true Korean saying. Sometimes these days, a bride's family has to sell their house to pay the dowry. Of course, the richness of the dowry depends on the groom's family. Generally, the bride has to buy western clothes for all her groom's male relatives, including his immediate family, his uncles on both sides, his male cousins and his grandparents. She must buy Korean clothes and sometimes western clothes as well, for all his female relatives. Then she prepares special gifts, including expensive jewellery, for her future mother-in-law, and she buys expensive quilted blankets for some of her husband's family members.

A groom, dressed in Korean traditional wedding clothes, carries a duck which symbolises fidelity and happiness.

Besides gifts to the groom's family, the bride's family also provides the furnishings for their new home. As more appliances have become available in Korea, this is an expensive affair: a stove, refrigerator, washing machine and even a television set or sound system are included.

The groom's family also prepares gifts for the bride's family, such as clothes and jewellery, but these are usually less expensive than those from the bride's family. If the bride's family is not providing a house, as few families can afford it, and if the newlyweds will not be living with the man's parents, as many do, then the groom's family is responsible for providing a home. The costs of the wedding ceremony and reception are equally divided between the two families.

It must be noted that while this is the general custom, there are many variations, depending on the family. For example, if the groom is from a prestigious but temporarily impoverished family, his family may give few gifts. Or, if the young couple is planning to go abroad to study, the groom's parents may ask that the bride's family helps with educational expenses rather than buying furnishings.

These gifts are exchanged before the actual wedding. Although the new couple will clearly belong to the man's family, the two families try to meet and establish amicable relations.

The Hahm

Hahm has a long tradition in Korea and some women today despise this custom. Others think it is a fun, though invariably noisy practice. Shortly before the wedding, the groom's friends carry the gifts from the groom's family to the bride's home in a wooden box, called a *hahm*. The time of delivery is pre-arranged with the bride's family. A friend of the groom who has had a son, or if no such friend exists, the largest friend, acts as a 'horse'. The 'horse' carries the box of gifts on his back and, true to his role, cannot speak. Another friend acts as a leader, directing the horse to go or stay.

They arrive at the bride's front gate and announce the horse is so tired that the bride's family must pay a certain amount of money for each step it takes. The women from the bride's family and the leader negotiate each step, the former having to pay money as each step is taken. It is a very noisy affair, as the groom's friends are a little drunk, and the playful bartering can go on for quite some time, to the amusement of the neighbours. Even if the bride's family lives in a modern high-rise apartment, the hahm can be carried up the many steps in this manner.

The men are greeted at the bride's front door by the bride's family, and inside by the bride and groom. Delicious food is prepared in advance, but the friends are usually more interested in using half the money collected to go out drinking. The other half they give to the young man as a

A bride in her white wedding dress.

wedding gift. A modern twist to this custom is for the bride to invite her friends to her house and, when the groom's friends go out to spend the money, they take the bride's friends with them to an expensive disco club. The bride and groom do not participate in this outing.

The Wedding Day

On the morning of the wedding, it is most common for the bride to go to a beauty parlour to be made up. Such a make-up job can transform the simplest young girl into a sophisticated model. No Korean bride looks anything but stunning. Her white, western style bridal gown is usually rented from the wedding hall, and she arrives at the hall just before the ceremony begins.

As weddings are important, friends and family make every effort to attend. Wedding halls are especially busy during the autumn and spring, when the guests of one wedding meet the guests of another coming in or going out, as the wedding hall schedules multiple weddings in one day. Two tables are set up to collect money, one for monetary gifts from the bride's guests, and the other for those of the groom's guests. Money is the standard wedding gift, and a close and trusted relative carefully guards the collection.

Most weddings are held at wedding halls, where a professor or distinguished friend or relative will preside, giving the couple useful advice about their marriage. The guests may talk during the ceremony, at least those who have managed to get into the overcrowded hall. If the wedding is held in a church, the pastor or priest presides.

During the ceremony, only the bride, groom and the person conducting the ceremony stand in front. It is standard to have bubbles surround the couple at some point during the ceremony. When the ceremony ends,

The bride and groom in traditional Korean clothes.

the newly-weds bow to each other and then to all the guests.

After the ceremony, photographs are taken. Then the couple quickly changes into traditional Korean wedding attire. The bride's costume includes a blouse in green and a skirt in red, the colours of the wedding hanbok and a beautiful gold crown; the groom wears an embroidered blue robe. In these cumbersome clothes, the couple bows deeply to the groom's parents and other relatives. The couple drinks a toast, called *pay beck*, to their new marriage and to the groom's family.

The Reception

Reception styles are almost as varied as the Koreans giving them. Most are lavish and the food is tasty, bountiful and beautiful. Rice cakes are always served as are noodles. Family and friends sit together talking and laughing as they celebrate the new couple's life together.

A Wedding: What to Expect

It is likely that you will be invited to a wedding while you are in Korea. Invitations are sometimes sent out, but verbal invitations are more common. Koreans think that asking someone to attend a wedding directly is almost like asking for money; and asking for money is not polite. So, as with other social events in Korea, you probably will not get much advance notice. In fact, the invitation may not come directly from the couple or their family. If you hear of the wedding from others, you are more than welcome to attend. The Korean for congratulations on your marriage is 'Kyul hon ul chook ha hahm ni da.'

The Honeymoon

Many weddings are held in the spring and autumn, when honeymooners can take advantage of the beautiful Korean scenery. The traditional honeymoon destination was Cheju Island, where a taxi driver would drive the young couple to see the sights and double as a photographer. Another favourite spot was Mt Sorak, nestled against the eastern coast. Today wealthier couples may go to Australia or Hawaii. Honeymoons generally last for three to seven days. When

Shopping for a traditional Korean dress.

the couple returns, they traditionally spend the first night in the bride's home and then move to the groom's home. Now most couples move into their own flat.

Koreans almost always give money instead of a gift, and it is appropriate for expatriates to do the same. The amount depends on the social status of the families and your own relationship to them. The minimum is 30,000 won, and only in exceptional cases would you give as much as 100,000 won. The money should be offered in an envelope, with a congratulatory message written on the front, and your name on the back.

If you wish to bring your spouse, children or a special friend, feel free to do so. Since the families involved will be tied up with the wedding, and most other guests will be unable to speak your native language, you would find it more interesting if you go with a friend or family member.

Working Life

Working in a Korean company is not easy. Much is expected of workers and long working hours are the norm. For example, many Koreans stay at the office until 10:00 pm. Koreans feel pride in obtaining a job at a large, well-known company. Work colleagues become an important part of one's life as one regularly socialises well into the night with one's co-workers.

Working mothers in Korea carry a double burden of being a worker and parent. Few childcare facilities exist and they are considered to be inferior to care by a family member. The best option is having grandparents provide care. Some women who expect to have a demanding professional career decide not to have children. The government, concerned about the low birthrate, is beginning to look at ways to provide support for families with working mothers.

Old Age

One of the main values of Confucianism is respect for the elderly. In Korea it is clear, just by seeing them walk around, that the elderly feel pride and a kind of self-respect that is not seen in older people in western societies. Many Koreans are surprised by how the elderly are treated other places. Like other aspects of Korean life, old age is changing. The number of Koreans living into their seventies and eighties has markedly increased, and though older Koreans are more independent than their ancestors, they continue to feel loved and cared for.

On the street in Korea, all elderly people are called *halmoni* (grandmother) or *halabuji* (grandfather), even though there are no blood ties. Seats on buses are invariably given up for an older person, and the visit of a grandparent to another city entails the preparation of special food and a big gathering of relatives.

The elderly compensate for their high-pressure youth and working life by taking leisurely trips. At famous tourist sites throughout the country, you will see groups of 20 or 30 elderly women, sometimes wearing their pastel hanboks, some perhaps leaning on canes. Women at this age are free to smoke or drink, as they never could in their youth. Similar groups of old men may be seen with their horsehair hats, visiting places they had no time to see in their younger days.

Hwangap

Traditionally, old age began when one reached 61 (this is 60 years in the western way of determining age). According to

Elderly Korean men, some most comfortable in traditional attire, can be seen frequently in the countryside and in the city.

the Chinese lunar calendar, every year in the cycle of 60 years (the sexagenary cycle) has a different name. The 12 animal years go through five cycles so after 60 years the cycle of 60 names begins again. On one's 61st birthday, the calendar has travelled a full cycle back to the birth year. Hwangap means that one is starting the cycle over again.

Modern medicine and improved living conditions have raised life expectancy to well past 60, and people continue to work beyond this age, but the 61st birthday is still an important event in a Korean's life.

On this day, the family prepares an especially large feast, often costing thousands of US dollars. Friends and relatives gather throughout the day to congratulate the honoured person and enjoy special delicacies, including rice cakes and fresh fruit of the season, and a commemorative photograph is taken.

Show Respect

It would be wise to follow the Korean custom of treating the old with respect. Upon entering a Korean home, the first person to greet is the oldest. Elder Koreans have mellowed with age, and the strict code of conduct has also been relaxed, so if they find you strange, they will stare and point you out more freely than their younger counterparts. They will also probably enjoy your company more, and accept your strange ways more readily.

With an expanding life span, most Koreans live not only to their 61st birthday but to their 71st and even longer. Each of these birthdays is cause for a big celebration. Some Koreans today choose to make the 61st birthday less important than years past, fully expecting to celebrate the 71st and perhaps the 81st birthday.

If you are over 60 yourself, and quite independent, you might dislike being treated as an old person. You would probably prefer a little less respect in exchange for being considered a useful member of society. Try to accept their respect graciously and remember it was not very long ago that few Koreans actually reached the age of 60; relative to that, you are among Korean society's venerable elders.

Death

Korean customs surrounding death are primarily derived from the Confucian value of respect for parents and ancestors. Koreans prefer to die at home. Every effort is made by doctors and nurses at hospitals to notify the family before a critically ill patient dies, so that he can be transported home. It is bad luck to bring the body of a deceased person home.

A deceased person is dressed in white hemp cloth and laid in a coffin. If the death occurred at home, the coffin is placed in the most honoured room, the master bedroom. If, unfortunately, the person died in hospital, the body will remain there and the wake takes place at the hospital. At either place, a screen usually hides the coffin from view. In front of the screen is a small, low table holding a photograph of the deceased and an incense burner.

Funeral Donations

When someone you know or the relative of someone you know dies, it is appropriate to visit the deceased. No gift is necessary, but you may give a little money (between 20,000 and 50,000 won) in an envelope. Korean stationary shops have special envelopes for his occasion. Donations are made at a table inside the home or hospital room. You can express condolences, burn incense and, if you wish, bow to the photograph of the deceased.

Many come to comfort the family and pay respect to the deceased. Guests are immediately escorted to the master bedroom, where they bow to the sons and once again, more deeply, before the photograph. Incense is burned. After they leave the room, they are served with refreshments.

The body usually remains at home for three days, sometimes as long as seven, depending on the social position of the deceased. Women usually do not stay close to the body, but spend this time cooking to feed the many visitors. The deceased's favourite food is prepared for him, as if he were able to eat it.

After the wake, unless cremation is chosen, the body is taken to the burial site. Traditionally, the women of the house served the deceased a final meal and said goodbye at home. These days, women sometimes accompany male relatives and friends to the burial site, which is usually on a mountain and, whenever possible, facing south. Husbands and wives are buried beside each other, and many families have graveyards where sons and their wives can be buried near their parents. Unlike western graves, the dirt covering them is shaped in a rounded mound.

Once at the burial site, the family and friends perform an ancestral ceremony. There is sometimes argument over which direction the body should be placed. The eldest son throws the first dirt over the coffin.

It is tragic if a son dies before his parents, particularly if he has no children. If there are no descendants to care for the grave, as is the case for all unmarried people, the body is cremated and the ashes often spread over a river or on a mountain.

Another exception to customary burial is the Buddhist funeral, where the body is cremated.

Few expatriates attend funerals, but if you are especially close to the deceased or the family, there is no harm in going. The ceremony is held at home and a rented bus will carry the body, family and friends to the burial site.

Ancestral Ceremonies

The custom of ceremonies to honour deceased relatives came to Korea from China even before Confucianism. It was reinforced when Confucianism became a major force influencing social behaviour. The ceremonies stressed filial piety and helped strengthen the bonds between living family members.

As with other customs in Korea, ancestral ceremonies vary widely, depending on the particular family customs, religion, and on the home of the first known family ancestor, who may have lived thousands of years ago. The ceremonies are so complex that many Koreans cannot say for sure what their particular family customs require on these important ceremonies.

Ceremonies At The Grave

Ceremonies are performed in front of the grave when the body is buried. They are then regularly performed in the spring (Hanshik Day), autumn (Chusok) and sometimes at whichever New Year the family celebrates. The oldest living male descendant is the leader responsible for the ceremony.

The line-up (above) for the traditional bow (below) before the ancestral graves. Notice that in this most respectful form, the heads almost touch the ground.

On the designated day, the male descendants (and sometimes their wives) go to the graves of their parents and grandparents, which are usually located next to each other. A small, low table or special cloth is placed in front of the graves and special food is set on it. Red food is placed towards the east, white towards the west.

Traditionally the leader bows twice before the table. These ancestral bows require that one lowers one's head to the ground. He then pours a glass of rice wine over the grave and bows twice with the other male descendants. Finally, the women, if any are present, bow two or four times. Bowing an odd number of times is unlucky. Sometimes families today vary the protocol, with men and women bowing at the same time.

After the initial bowing, the graves and surrounding areas are cleaned up. Grass is cut and flowering plants are sometimes planted. Twenty or thirty minutes later, the bowing ceremony is repeated. The offering of food and alcohol is then consumed. Though the ceremony is serious, it is not sad. It is a time for the descendants to remember their ancestors, to pay respect, and to feel the importance and bonding of the current family. Children sometimes attend, and though they are required to be quiet, it is an enjoyable occasion for them, not unlike a picnic.

Ceremonies In The Home

Ancestral ceremonies are held at the home of the oldest surviving male, three or four times a year: on the death anniversary, on New Year's Day, Chusok and, for the first three years after the death, on the deceased's birthday. The home ceremony is similar to the graveyard one, except that bowing is before a photograph of the ancestor instead of the grave.

Notable Exceptions

When Christian missionaries came to Korea, they forbade ancestral ceremonies as a form of idolatry. Today most Christians do hold some kind of ceremony but it is far simpler than the traditional ceremony. Churches are divided on the issue. When Korea had primarily an agricultural economy, sons lived near each other and near to the family graves. It was easy for them to perform the ceremonies many times each year. This is of course no longer possible.

Regional Differences

Though Korea is a homogeneous country compared to most countries in the world, Koreans make some clear distinctions about people coming from or living in different regions of Korea. The primary difference is between those living in the Seoul area and those not. People in Seoul (about 25 per cent of Korea's population), like most people living in the capital city, consider it the only place to live and believe that people who live down in the provinces to be somewhat uncultured and backward. Accents identify people who live outside of Seoul and people in Seoul report that people from the provinces speak loudly, as if they are yelling all the time. Seoulites certainly do have more international exposure and Seoulites see foreigners on a daily basis.

People in the provinces resent the backward impression Seoulites have of them. People outside Seoul consider themselves to be more open and friendly, and expatriates living in the provinces would agree. Though Seoul does have access to the latest technology and fashion first, with national TV and the short distances between any two places in Korea, people in the provinces are months, not years, behind their Seoul counterparts. People in the provinces are rightly proud of their cleaner air and lighter traffic. Teachers in provinces sometimes refuse to be transferred to Seoul, where, they believe, teachers are less respected and parents more demanding.

Besides the distinction between Seoul and the provinces, there are, naturally, differences between the provinces and these are reflected particularly in language and diet. The southwest (Cholla) provinces and southeast (Gyungnam) provinces eat hotter and spicier food, as their milder climate required heavier spices to preserve kimchee throughout the winter. Accents from people from these two provinces are quite distinct so people moving to Seoul from these regions are easily identified. There has also been a long history of tension between people from these two provinces, sometimes taken advantage of by politicians in past decades.

In recent years, more refugees from North Korea have moved to South Korea (usually via China). While South Koreans are pleased that their fellow Koreans are able to escape the difficult life in the north, integrating these refugees into the south has not been without problems. The refugees are generally young and come without family and this lack of supervision comes with problems. Attempts to assimilate these youth into regular Korean schools have not be successful.

SOCIALISING

CHAPTER 4

'To know a stream, one must wade through it;
to know a man, one must associate with him.'
—A Korean Proverb

Most Koreans welcome the opportunity to learn about other cultures and share their traditions with from people from other countries. It works best when one is introduced or when one meets a Korean in the context of one's daily life. It is important to understand that Korean rules are different from yours, and equally important to realise that patience and good humour will take you a long way, as will a general knowledge of Korean culture and customs. Still, Koreans are quick to forgive foreigners their mistakes, particularly when it is clear that the expatriate is trying to understand and learn Korean customs. This chapter begins with an explanation of introductions, and moves on to communication between expatriates and Koreans. Koreans make a clear distinction between strangers and acquaintances, so this topic will be explored as will be the meaning of Korean friendships. Since it is valuable to understand how Koreans view particular groups of expatriates this chapter will summarise some of the impressions Koreans generally have towards particular groups of expatriates. The final section of this chapter will discuss relationships which cross gender and culture.

INTRODUCTIONS

Introductions are not taken lightly in Korea. In many western countries, if two people happen to be at the same place at the same time with a mutual friend, the latter will casually introduce them. In Korea, an introduction called *So gae* permanently changes the way two people relate to each other in the future. Introducing a person of relatively little status to someone of higher status is uncommon.

Before two people meet for the first time, their mutual friend will probably give both some background information on the person they are about to meet. When they actually meet, there is a ritual which is invariably followed. If one person is sitting when another (standing) is to be introduced, the former will stand up. This is true of women and of men. One person will say something like 'This is my first time to see you.' The other will make a similar statement. They will then face each other directly, bow and say their names. 'Cho eum boeb ket seum ni da' is the Korean for 'How do you do'; *Man na byoe-o pan kahp seum ni da'* is 'I am glad to meet you'.

It is sometimes difficult to hear the names as they are bowing, but that does not matter as, following the bow, business cards are exchanged. This gives both a better idea of their status in relation to each other. Men often shake hands at this point, sometimes extending two hands to show respect for the other person.

Knowing a person's status is critical, since the proper language level to be used depends on the two people's positions. Until they know, they will both use very formal, respectful language.

Once introduced, they can talk. Much of the early conversation will consist of personal questions, seeking some connection that will make them feel closer. If their names are the same, they will ask for the origin of the name. For example, if the two people turn out to be the same 'Kim' (such as Kimhae Kim, meaning one's early ancestors came from the city of Kimhae), they will quickly warm to each other. Other common factors sought are previous schools attended, home town and hobbies. If one person is obviously older than the other, he will begin addressing the younger in more intimate language.

Rarely do Koreans introduce themselves to someone with whom they have no connection. It does sometimes happen that two people strike up a conversation, perhaps sitting

Never forget the importance of introductions. Though you may feel uncomfortable not introducing your wife or a friend who is with you when you chance upon a colleague on the street, in some situations it might better not to burden your colleague with an introduction. Also, do not ask to be introduced to someone unless you have a particular reason to want to know him.

next to each other on a long bus ride, or when a query leads to a longer conversation. Before they part, one will say 'I guess we don't know one another's names.' They will then say their names, bow and exchange cards. A future relationship will have been established.

It goes without saying that you must never run out of name cards which state your name, company and exact title. If possible, have the information written in Korean on one side of your card. Have a system for organising other people's name cards for your easy reference. Once you have been introduced, you can call and ask for assistance of any kind.

Koreans place their family names before their given names, but when introducing themselves to foreigners, they often follow the western custom of placing the family name after the given name.

COMMUNICATION

Many Koreans like to talk to foreigners. Some, especially those who have travelled abroad, will approach an expatriate, eager to make him or her feel comfortable. But most Koreans are reserved compared to westerners. Some are embarrassed by their poor language skills, and some, especially from rural parts of Korea, just do not know what to make of a stranger, especially one from a strange land.

PERSONAL QUESTIONS

In getting to know one another, Koreans will often ask quite personal questions. It is usual to ask someone if he or she is married, and if not, why not? If married, for how long? If no children, why not? Why did you get divorced?

Except for much older women, asking someone their age is not considered impolite. Questions about how much your home or watch are worth are a normal part of Korean conversations. Such questions are not intended to embarrass you. Many expatriates find that Koreans ask them more personal questions than they would ask other Koreans.

There is no obligation to answer questions if you are not so inclined. Your conversation partner's primary concern is usually that you feel comfortable. If you consider a question too personal, answer humorously and change the subject, or pretend that you didn't hear. Try not to reveal feeling offended.

SMALL TALK

Personal questions can be suitable small talk when interacting with Koreans. You can ask for details of someone's job, but be sensitive if he wishes to reveal only basic facts. Koreans often ask about hobbies, and you can do the same. Men enjoy talking about their military experiences (nearly all men serve for two years). Women can be asked about their children. People who have travelled find it interesting to discuss where they have been. As most Koreans are well-read about national and international events, current news can be discussed, keeping in mind that until you know the person well, criticisms of Korea, even the Korean government, will not be well received. You can, however, freely criticize the customs or government of your own country.

Koreans are eager to hear your opinion about anything Korean. They are very pleased to hear which foods you like, what places you have visited in Korea, how Korea favourably compares to other places you have lived, and how kind and polite Koreans are. Such statements, if sincere, are sure to increase the *kibun* of any Korean.

SENSITIVE TOPICS

In the interest of making you comfortable and keeping harmony, Koreans are careful to anticipate how you will respond to a question or comment and will generally avoid topics that may make you embarrassed or cause uneasiness. For example, if it is not clear that someone went to the university, one would not ask this questions, as she or he may feel uncomfortable revealing that she or he did not go. Likewise, when disagreement or criticism is necessary,

Koreans generally couch it in agreements or compliments. For example, if you must say you do not like *kimchee*, at the same time note that you like several other Korean foods.

Koreans will not talk much about their families, especially if there has been some trouble or a death. Anything related to adoption or being divorced is carefully avoided (though sometimes foreigners are asked about these things). In the past it was considered boastful to say anything good about one's wife or children, and though this is changing, Koreans are still modest about their immediate family. They would particularly minimise their family members' accomplishments if it made your family, by comparison, look bad.

Koreans are sensitive to your feelings about a subject, and you would be wise to be equally sensitive to theirs. If they do not wish to discuss something, they may smile at your question and say nothing. Or they may appear uncomfortable and try to change the subject.

To many expatriates, it seems that Koreans are particularly sensitive to criticism of Korea. You will be asked hundreds of times about your first impression of Korea, and how you like living here. Strongly negative comments will not be taken well. Koreans are proud of their heritage and their country. Anyone bold enough to judge these negatively would not be viewed favourably.

REFUSING OFFERS OF DRINK AND FOOD

In the spirit of humility, Koreans generally refuse offers of food or drink one or more times. The expatriate should not take these refusals at face value as they might in their own country. Be sure to offer a second of third time, knowing that the initial refusals may simply mean they are being polite, not wanting to appear too eager. When you are offered something to eat or drink, you can accept initially as Koreans know foreigners are more direct. You can also follow the Korean custom of not accepting the first invitation. If you really do not want something, and honestly refuse, you can expect to be asked again and again, despite your best protests.

NON-VERBAL COMMUNICATION

Although some nonverbal behaviour is universal like blushing and laughing, some of it is unique to each culture. Nonverbal communication can support, emphasise or contradict what one says verbally. Many expatriates in Korea find that much communication that would be stated verbally in their own countries is communicated nonverbally in Korea.

For example, when one is riding a bus or underground train with a heavy load of books, and there is no seat, it is common for a seated person to offer to hold the books. The offer includes no verbal sound. The seated person merely tugs at the books until the holder realises he is not trying to steal them, but is actually offering to hold them. At first, many expatriates think Koreans communicate nonverbally because they assume the foreigner knows no Korean. If you observe Koreans in the same situation, however, you will notice that they communicate with each other non-verbally as well. For Koreans, it is awkward to talk to someone who has not been introduced, and this nonverbal communication is comfortable for all concerned.

Some other examples of non-verbal communication are described below.

Bowing

One of the first things visitors to Korea notice is the bowing. The bow can symbolise many things, and is performed by each person many times a day.

When one Korean meets another for the first time in a day, it is appropriate to bow and say '*Annyong haseyo*'. The person of lower status should bow and say this first, and the other should respond quickly with the same bow and greeting. If the other person has a much greater status, such as that between father and child, he does not bow, but uses intimate language in the greeting. You can guess the relative status of two people by the way they greet each other. A teacher and his

Anyone can bow, but getting it exactly right is more difficult than it seems. Learning to bow may be like learning a language – if it is not done before one reaches adolescence, it can never be done perfectly. Practice does not seem to help. Expatriates always look a little strange bowing.

student, an employer and his employee, an uncle and his niece are all easily distinguished by their bows.

A Korean bows when introduced to someone for the first time. The introducer briefly presents the two people to each other; one of them bows and softly says his own name, and the other responds in the same manner. Name cards are then exchanged, face up, since it is difficult to hear the names, and this will give each person more information about the other, as well as his position.

Koreans bow when they part. This time they say (to the one leaving) '*Annyonghi gaseyo*' and (to the one staying) '*Annyonghi gyeseyo*.' Translated literally, these mean 'Go (or stay) in peace.' Koreans are all familiar with the English 'goodbye' and tend to use it when speaking to expatriates.

Some more unique forms of bowing are reserved for special occasions, particularly when one wants to show an unusual degree of respect. In the most respectful kind, the Korean lowers his or her head all the way to the ground, and touches both palms to the floor. This is done after a marriage ceremony, at ancestors' graves and during the New Year celebrations.

The Perfect Nude Bow

Recently my mother visited me in Korea, where I was teaching English. I wanted her to experience the jimjilbang-the public showers and saunas. We were also planning to meet a close friend of mine later that evening at the jimjilbang, so we decided to get on with the showers, and undressed and entered the wet saunas. We were broiling ourselves, when I finally spotted my friend entering the room, and not until that moment did I consider that we probably should have arranged to meet each other clothed. But no one was inordinately embarrassed, as is the nature of these public showers, and my mother and my friend greeted each other in the nude. The curious thing is that though we, and everyone else in the room were naked, my friend still inadvertently bowed in the proper Korean greeting. She didn't even notice that she'd done it: the perfect nude bow.

Bowing in the right circumstances, however, no matter how clumsily, will be well received by Koreans. It shows that you are trying (no matter if unsuccessfully) to fit into their culture. Actually, even for a foreigner, bowing seems to be the natural thing to do in response to another's bow. Some expatriates who spend most of their time around Koreans even find themselves bowing to other westerners.

PERSONAL SPACE

Personal space is a rare commodity in Korea. This is natural in a country with one of the highest population densities in the world. Koreans are used to sleeping, working, eating and standing in conditions that would be considered far too crowded by many westerners. Even in smaller towns throughout Korea, buildings are close together. The imaginary bubble of air that many expatriates like having around them will be intruded upon regularly in Korea.

This invasion of personal space can be a source of irritation for expatriates. Walking on the street, standing in a lift, working with other people in an office or visiting the local market can all become affronts to one's personal space. After living in Korea a while, expatriates get mostly used to the close encounters but there is stress nonetheless.

Expatriates who have lived in Korea report that the lack of respect for others has improved significantly, perhaps in response to a citizenship campaign held before the 2002 World Cup. Koreans used to push to get into a lift, before those leaving could get out. This is rare to see in metropolitan areas of Korea. Now, instead of pushing to get on the underground, they wait for others to get off and may even let another person on before them. During rush hour, however, pushing is required if only to fit on the train.

When a Korean inadvertently bumps into someone or steps on another's foot in public, he is unlikely to apologise. This is not unique to foreigners as Koreans are even less likely to apologise to another Korean. This is probably related to the awkwardness Koreans feel in talking to someone they do not have not been introduced to.

PHYSICAL CONTACT BETWEEN MEN AND WOMEN

According to Confucian custom, boys and girls should be separated from the age of five. A generation ago, schools were segregated so that few boys and girls had any friends of the opposite sex. Traditionally, physical contact between boy and girl was prohibited until after marriage. Overt affection was reserved for the privacy of one's own room. Today it is not uncommon to see affection between young men and women expressed in public, such as on an underground train or in a park. Couples are less likely to demonstrate their affection among people that they know.

CONTACT BETWEEN PEOPLE OF THE SAME GENDER

More common than physical contact between couples is physical contact between close friends of the same gender.

Don't Be Shy

A Korean generally will not touch another of the same sex unless he feels particularly friendly with that person. If someone grabs your hand or puts his hand on your leg, it is a an indication of caring and friendship. If it makes you very uncomfortable, there is no need to endure it; simply tell your friend that in your country such behaviour has a different meaning, and you would rather he did not touch you. Few Koreans would be offended by a sensible statement such as this.

It is common to see two women walking hand in hand. In a crowded classroom, one man may sit on another man's lap, seeming to enjoy the friendly, physical contact. Male friends may sit for some time with the arm of one on the thigh of the other. To Koreans, physical contact is a natural way to show their feelings to whom one feels especially close. Depending on the country that one comes from, this may be awkward to the expatriate. Other expatriates come to appreciate the warmth and care that Koreans express through physical affection.

EYE CONTACT

Most people are not conscious of their own culture's pattern of eye contact until they run into someone who follows a different pattern. Typical westerners will maintain eye contact throughout a conversation, glancing away only briefly, with the listener keeping better eye contact than the speaker. Not to look at someone 'in the eye' is considered disrespectful or suspicious. When being scolded, it is disrespectful to not look at a person of higher status.

In Korea, eye contact is kept about half the time during a conversation. When not looking at the other person, the Korean looks to either side, rather than up or down. Koreans of higher status generally keep longer eye contact than those of lower status. When one or both are angry, or during a business transaction, long eye contact is maintained. If a Korean is being scolded, he will look down slightly. People of lower status should not stare too long at someone of higher status.

GESTURES

Some gestures confuse the foreigner in Korea. The Korean 'come' is similar to the western 'goodbye'. When an expatriate waves goodbye from a distance, the Korean may think he is being asked to come. Koreans wave goodbye by waving their arm from side to side. The western version of 'come', holding palm upward, is used by Koreans only when calling a dog.

Koreans always use the right hand when handing any object to a person of higher status. To show more respect, the left hand is put, palm up, just below the elbow to support the right arm. To show the most respect, both hands hold the object as it is given or received. If a child shows a tendency to prefer his left hand, his parents and teachers will strongly encourage him to change to his right hand, as right-handed behaviour is considered most polite.

When Koreans are happy, they smile and laugh as people do the world over. But smiling holds another special meaning in Korea. It is common for a Korean to smile when he feels ashamed or uncomfortable. If your maid drops your antique crystal vase, she is likely to smile, aggravating the unenlightened westerner further.

Traditionally, women were supposed to cover their mouths whenever they laughed or smiled. Today this is not always done, but most expatriates will still see it happen from time to time.

SILENCE

Koreans seem to be more comfortable with silence than westerners. Two friends can enjoy each other's company without speaking for long periods. Strong feelings are sensed; stating deep emotions is thought to make their meaning trivial. Eating may also be done in silence, as the enjoyment of a meal is believed to require one's complete attention.

KNOCKING ON DOORS

In Korea it is considered impolite to enter a room without giving some notice. Traditionally, people cleared their throats to indicate their presence. Today, they are more likely to knock on the door. If a secretary gives you permission to enter her boss' room which has a closed or even partially open door, you should not walk right in. It is considerate to knock first, twice or thrice rapidly. There is no need to wait for the person to come to the door or to respond. An expatriate can

Tips for Non-Verbal Communication

- Koreans communicate much non-verbally; through gestures, facial expressions, body language
- Physical contact between people of the same gender is common in Korea
- Koreans have less physical contact between people of different genders
- Physical contact between western men and Korean women particularly should be minimised
- Pointing is considered rude by Koreans
- Koreans notice that westerners use many gestures while talking
- 'Come' is communicated with palm down, hand parallel to floor
- Don't write names in red (red is only used for names of dead people)
- Personal space different; in general, Koreans require less than Americans

expect the same behaviour towards himself. If your door is closed and someone wants to see you, he or she will knock and then enter. Do not expect people to wait until you open the door or tell them to enter.

This custom is especially noticeable in public toilets. Sometimes the lock does not work, or there may not even be one. When a door is closed, it is polite to knock first. If someone is inside, he will knock back, or make a noise so that you know not to enter. Do the same if you do not want your toilet privacy to be invaded. Clearing one's throat loudly will communicate equally well.

REFRAIN FROM WEARING SHOES IN HOMES

Koreans never wear shoes in the home. To wear shoes in a Korean home would be insensitive at best and insulting at worst. Korean homes are designed to accommodate family member and guest shoes in the entry-way. Leaving shoes there keeps the street dirt out of the home. For this reason, shoes that can be put on and taken off easily are ideal to wear when visiting Korean homes. Socks without holes should be worn. Many expatriates living in Korea also find themselves reducing or eliminating shoes in their home while living in Korea, some continuing this custom when they return to their own countries. It does keep one's home much cleaner. Koreans coming to your home, including service people and guests, will be uncomfortable wearing shoes in your home.

A Question of Culture

When Korean workers moved us into a new house I was surprised that not once did a mover wear his shoes in my home, despite my insistence that it was okay. Even when they carried in a heavy wardrobe or full-sized couch, each worker in turn, left their shoes at the door as they entered my new home and slipped their shoes back on as they headed out for the next load.

STRANGERS AND ACQUAINTANCES

One thing that puzzles new expatriates in Korea is how differently people are treated in different situations. The newly arrived foreign business person will be shown extreme politeness and kindness, even though he is meeting business people for the first time. But later, as he tries to catch a taxi, he may be pushed aside, and even stepped on, without so much as a word of apology. The two types of behaviour contradict each other. Koreans can be both extremely polite and extremely rude!

Strangers

In Korea, a person to whom one has not been introduced, with whom one has had no previous interactions, nor foresees any future relationship, is not a person requiring the careful respect and kindness Koreans show those they know. When Koreans lived in small agricultural villages everyone was connected to everyone else, including people they had never met. So everyone followed the strict Korean rules of etiquette, even when dealing with strangers. Then people moved to large cities, where there were no particular connections with others.

With little money, time or energy, and an abundance of people who had a claim on their resources, it was impossible for Koreans to treat everyone properly, in the old way. Perhaps the only way to avoid helping and giving respect to the hundreds of needy strangers on the street, was to pretend that they did not exist. To recognise their existence was to treat them generously and politely.

Another reason was the anonymity of cities: dishonest people could steal and cheat without being labelled for the rest of their lives. It became dangerous to trust others or to act kindly. Strangers came to be viewed as people 'out to get you', people who did not consider others worthy of respect.

Acquaintances

Most of the people a Korean has any regular contact with are considered worthy of proper treatment. Past and present neighbours, those who provide services, teachers (his or hers and those of people he or she knows), anyone who has attended the same schools—all of these automatically fit into this category.

People working in the same company, though never introduced, are also considered part of this sphere of human relationships. Friends and anyone a friend has introduced also deserve proper treatment.

In reality, there are hundreds, perhaps thousands of people in one's life who deserve proper treatment. These relationships require an enormous amount of time, money and psychological energy. It would seem almost impossible to treat all those people in the same way. Yet those hundreds of people connected to a Korean are treated with kindness, humbleness and due respect.

Until rather recently, people in the homogenous Korean society had few chances to see foreigners, who are still somewhat novel to many Koreans. One Korean misconception is that non-Koreans cannot understand their language, so when they say something about a foreigner in his presence, they imagine he will not understand. As an expatriate in Korea, you may be pointed at, your clothes and hairstyle analysed, and your figure evaluated, all in your presence. As one expatriate commented, it is as though you were a character on television, unaware of the attention and therefore undisturbed by it.

A Korean who has a relationship with an expatriate treats him with all the politeness that only 'real' persons deserve. In fact, except for talking about them in their presence, Koreans show more politeness to expatriates, even those they do not know, than they do to other Koreans. Sometimes that extra politeness may not always seem polite enough, but luckily, most of your time will be spent with people who do consider you a 'real' person, and who treat you with much more kindness than you would expect in your home country.

> In Korea, you will be treated very kindly by most of the Koreans you meet. Korea generally lives up to its reputation as the country of politeness. There will nevertheless be times when you will be treated as a 'non-person', and the experience of those occasions may stay with you for a long while.

FRIENDSHIP

In the Korean way of thinking, a real friend is as intimate as a family member. A friend cannot be made easily and, once made, must never be neglected. Koreans often view western friendships as fickle and shallow.

A friend is someone to relax with (relaxing is not as easy in a family setting), to listen to your problems, to truly understand you, and on whose generous help you can count at any time in your life-and vice versa. The most reliable friends are made early in life-during elementary, secondary school or college. Some Koreans believe that after that time one's heart cannot fully open to another human being. Some friends are made at university, but rarely are deep friendships formed after that.

Such friends will keep in touch through years of separation. The obligations are almost as great as those of a family member. People may give thousands of dollars to their less fortunate friends. A Korean who does not live up to his responsibility as an intimate friend would lose face among other friends. Like people of all cultures, there are different levels of intimacy among friends, with greater closeness and understanding and great obligations for some friends. Westerners are likely to be surprised how much Koreans will do even for less close friends.

There are also Koreans who welcome the relative openness of adults from other countries, and they respond by opening themselves, perhaps even more intimately than they would to their fellow Koreans. Expatriates with such relationships feel especially fortunate, for the deep kindness shown in such a friendship is more than they are likely to experience in their own country.

Relationships between Koreans and expatriates can fall into friendship patterns from either culture, or, more often, a combination of the two. Some Koreans will view the expatriate as someone to benefit from: a partner for conversation practice; a free temporary home if he visits the foreigner's homeland; a means of obtaining a visa to that country. Some expatriates have felt used, not realising that many relationships between Koreans are also established primarily for utilitarian reasons.

No matter what kind of friendship exists between a Korean and yourself, it will enrich your stay in Korea; having only expatriate friends, one is isolated from the real Korea. Sometimes the most natural friendships between the two cultures arise between expatriates and Koreans who have lived in the expatriates' country, and who are thus sympathetic to the difficulties of living outside one's culture. Koreans who have lived abroad also often understand expatriates' frustrations with some aspects of Korean life.

HOW DIFFERENT GROUPS OF FOREIGNERS ARE VIEWED BY KOREANS

Koreans are well exposed to western media so many of their images of other people are conceived through movies and television, primarily originating in the United States. Anyone with light skin will be assumed to be 'American' or from the United States. Expatriates of other citizenship find that their non-U.S. citizenship is generally viewed favourably. While Koreans in general are not pleased with recent actions of the United States government, this is not generally held against people they perceive to be from the United States. Besides the close connection the United States military has with their government, there have been regular, well-publicised incidences by U.S. military soldiers against Korean civilians, resulting in a somewhat negative view towards service men and women from the United States. Expatriates who are not associated with the U.S. military often choose to distance themselves from the military by their clothes or hairstyle.

Koreans have less knowledge and contact with people of African descent (whatever their citizenship may be) and may be initially fearful or uncomfortable around people with dark skin. While Korean business people appreciate tourists who come from Japan, in general Koreans attitudes towards the Japanese is not positive, given the problematic history of the two nations. Younger Koreans are less negative than older people who experienced Japanese occupation of their country.

People of Korean descent who have been adopted are in a unique situation in Korea. Koreans consider blood very important, so even though you may be an adoptee, if you have Korean birth parents, you are still considered part of the Korean family. However, Koreans may feel some shame that you were not cared for in your birth country and, surprisingly, may not appreciate that your parents did not teach you Korean. When a Korean-looking person speaks a small amount of Korean it is not always admired as it is when a western looking person speaks a bit of Korean.

Likewise, Koreans who were raised outside of Korea by Korean parents are viewed in a complex way. You, too, are part of the Korean family. Some Koreans feel more familiar with you than with other people coming from abroad. Others may be jealous of the opportunities you have enjoyed; and others may resent that you do not know your language and culture adequately. They initially will watch to see if you consider yourself better than Koreans born and raised in their own country. Koreans value humility in people of all situations.

Asians coming from countries such as the Philippines, China, Thailand, and Pakistan are generally in Korea to do low-skilled and poorly-paid labour. As such, they are given less status than other expatriates. Some expatriates coming from these countries find that they are treated as an inferior until their position is known.

In recent years, some women from Russia have come to Korea to work in the service industry. A young, western English teacher of European descent lived near one such brothel and was sometimes mistaken for a prostitute. Dress, behaviour and language can usually make it clear who you are.

Relationships that Cross Gender and Culture

Just as contact between Korean men and women has become more common in the last twenty years, and Koreans are likely to have romantic relationships with various partners before marrying, so have relationships between foreign people and Korean people of the opposite gender become more common and acceptable. There are, however, some cautions the expatriate may take as one enters into a potentially problematic and satisfying relationship with a Korean.

Early cross-cultural romantic relationships in Korea were largely between male soldiers from the United States and Korean women, often in the service industry. These relationships carried a negative stigma, and few families of high status would tolerate their daughter's involvement with a man from a western country. Far rarer were (and still are) relationships between Korean men and foreign women. These relationships generally were between educated men who had studied or worked abroad and met similarly educated women. These relationships carried little stigma. Since women join their husband's family at marriage, a foreign woman would become a member of her Korean husband's family; whereas when a Korean woman married a foreign man, she would be leaving the whole culture and be at the mercy of a foreign family.

Thankfully for the single expatriate living in Korea romantic relationships with Koreans are more acceptable today. Most Koreans have relatives who have spent significant time abroad and it is not uncommon for people to know someone who has ventured into an international marriage. Some Korean families would still be cautious about such relationships, particularly for their daughters. The intentions of an expatriate man will be watched carefully. Koreans think of westerners of both genders as being more sexual.

There are many opportunities for single expatriates to meet Koreans, particularly male expatriates. Work is an excellent way to meet people as are parties hosted by Korean friends. Koreans who are particularly interested in interacting with foreigners are likely to hang out in areas that foreigners frequent so those are good places to meet people. There are also on-line chat rooms and Internet dating services that focus on matching Koreans with expatriates, some of which are advertised in the English newspapers.

Relationships Between Gay and Lesbian Expatriates and Koreans

Until recently, most Koreans would have denied that homosexuals existed in their country. However, some popular and well-known Korean entertainers have recently come out; some continue to be successful and others have not. Another indication of Korea's growing awareness of alternative sexuality are the university clubs for gays, lesbians and others exploring their sexual identity. Though Koreans realise that they live among gays and lesbians, this does not mean homosexuality is free from stigma. As important as it is to conform to family expectations and to be accepted by one's peers, most Koreans who are gay marry and have children and discreetly have affairs. An area of Itaewon is known for its gay and lesbian bars. Expatriates who are gay or lesbians can certainly meet Korean and other expatriates who are gay or lesbian, but it would be wise to carry on these relationships as Koreans do; unobtrusively.

SETTLING IN & MANAGING CULTURE SHOCK

CHAPTER 5

'Weather one is well or woeful is
determined by one's mind.'
—A Korean Proverb

MOVING IS STRESSFUL and moving to a new culture has added complexities. There are, however, many things you can do to make this process easier for yourself and others who may be moving with you. This chapter will help prepare you for the transition to your life in Korea and provide you with valuable information about the particularities of Korean living to make your adjustment easier. This chapter will also examine culture shock, including how to minimise its effects and how it may be experienced by different groups of people

FORMALITIES
Visa
Depending on your nationality, you may be able to visit Korea for 90 days without a visa. To get a visa for a longer stay, or to work in Korea, you must apply for a Korean visa outside of Korea at a Korean embassy or consulate. There are many types of work visas. For example, an A-1 visa is for a diplomat, a D-2 visa is for a student, an E-2 visa is for an English Teacher and an F-1 visa is for a dependent. It is rarely possible to change your visa status without leaving the country. Changing from a dependent visa (e.g. if one is here with a working spouse) is particularly difficult and would result in the loss of privileges that are associated with that dependent visa. If one changes employers but has the same visa status, one must still leave Korea to change the sponsor of the visa, but this change can often be made quickly in Japan.

Working without the proper visa is forbidden. Resident visas must be renewed every year but one does not need to leave the country to renew a visa with the same employer.

Foreigner's Residence Certificate

Expatriates living in Korea must obtain a Residence Certificate. This is a complex process and requires multiple forms. Your workplace may be able to help you with this for all the members in your family. Like immigration offices in all countries, things often take longer than expected and require what seems like additional documents at each step of the process. Everyone must be fingerprinted. Patience and a sense of humour will serve you well.

Koreans register in the *dong* (neighbourhood) office where they live and when they change residence, marry etc. they must file papers at their respective neighbourhood office. As a foreigner, once you have your residency certificate, instead of registering in the neighborhood office you must register in the *gu* (district) office. Here again, Koreans at your workplace or a good Korean friend may need to assist you.

Required documents for a residence certificate:
- Application Form
- Passport
- Three photographs (taken within six months, 3x4cm)
- A fee of 10,000 won

Checklist for Before You Go
- Passports
- Visas
- Insurance for while you are abroad
- International driver's permit
- Medical records
- Prescriptions and medications
- School records
- Pet health and immunisation records
- Will and guardianships
- Power of attorney

- Bill paying arrangements
- Close unneeded accounts
- Inventory
- Copies of important documents (left with someone in your native country and carried with you)
- Passports
- Visas
- Driver's license, international driving permit
- Insurance information
- Change your address
- Banks
- Credit cards
- Stockbroker agent
- Lawyer
- Accountant
- Insurance company
- Tax offices
- Voter registration office
- Magazines and periodical
- Alumni association and professional memberships

LIVING ACCOMMODATION
Serviced Apartments

Service apartments are a good option for people with extended but not permanent stays in Korea, people waiting for their household goods to arrive and people needing time to look for permanent housing. Serviced apartments combine the advantages of hotel and apartment living. They come fully furnished, have kitchens, high-speed internet connections, phones, health clubs and restaurants. One can settle in quite comfortably and cook for oneself. Unlike renting standard houses or flats which require a hefty deposit, payment is made by the day, week or month.

Homestays

For single people, another option is a homestay with a Korean family. This can be for as short as a few days to longer than a year. Some organisations arrange such accommodation for their English teachers. This is an excellent way to become

familiar with Korean culture and to get to know Koreans quite well. It is usually cheaper to live in a homestay than to pay for your own home or flat. Friendships with homestay family members can ward against loneliness and provide assistance in managing a new culture. Most homestays develop into close and satisfying relationships but like all human interactions, can present challenges.

Permanent Housing

Most Koreans, including those of middle and upper income, live in individually owned apartment units in tall, cement apartment buildings. Those with less money live in very small units and those with abundant resources live in spacious units with multiple bathrooms, roomy kitchens, several balconies and numerous bedrooms. Housing developments usually include ten or many more buildings, each 15 to 20 storeys high. Since thousands of people live in one development it is not surprising that many conveniences, such as play grounds, dry-cleaners, schools and grocery shops, are located within the complex. Produce trucks often park outside such flats on a regular basis making it easy for residents to purchase fresh fruits and vegetables. Korean flats invariably are long and thin, with each apartment having windows on each side of the building. This allows for cross-ventilation. Flats are arranged, if at all possible, so that the master bedroom and living room are on the south side of the building. A second choice would be on the west side to allow for sun to shine on those rooms. Some Koreans live in townhouses or 'villas' which are similar to flats but not as tall. Many expatriates also live in such flats. Though from the outside they look impersonal and cold, inside they are comfortable, personal, and convenient.

Some very wealthy Koreans prefer to live in single family homes. Koreans consider it less convenient to live in a free standing home because vacant homes are invitations to thieves. Someone needs to be in the home at all times. Many expatriates, however, are accustomed to living in a single family home and some sponsoring businesses are willing to pay for such living accommodation. Homes have the advantage of a yard and greater privacy.

All houses and flats in Korea use a unique heating system that most expatriates like. The *ondol* heating system is a series of pipes with warm water that run underneath the rooms of the house, making the floors warm. Since Koreans traditionally ate, slept and sat on the floor, it kept everyone pleasingly warm. Expatriates find it wonderful to have warm floors to walk on in the midst of winter and it makes scientific sense as heat invariably rises, keeping the whole house at a pleasant temperature.

FINDING A HOME

Some companies find housing for their expatriate employees. More common is for them to allow you to choose your own, perhaps connecting you to a real estate agent accustomed to working with expatriates. Some companies pay for a look-see where one can find a home prior to moving to Korea. It is essential that you know how much money your employer (or you) is willing to spend as housing is quite costly. If you are going to Korea on your own, English language newspapers list the names of realtors who speak English. Some expatriates stay in hotels while they find permanent housing and when they are waiting for their household belongs to arrive. Some

A traditional style Korean home displayed at the Korean Folk Village. Such homes are no longer in use.

Korean real estate agents now hire an expatriate who lives in Korea to facilitate communication.

CHOOSING AN AREA TO LIVE IN

In most cities, there are areas with a high concentration of foreign residents. There are obvious advantages to living near other expatriates. It is pleasant to be near others who speak your language and who can give you support and advice. Supermarkets that cater to expatriates' tastes are conveniently located in these areas, softening the effects of a different culture. If you have children, being close to the school or the school bus line is likely to be an important factor in your choice. Traffic patterns and the location of your job are other things to consider.

In Seoul, people make a distinction between living north or south of the Han River. The older part of the city, north of the Han River, includes the city centre, and has roads that wind around mountains and go through tunnels. Gang Nam (south of the Han River) has wider roads that are spread out in a gridlock and has mostly newer buildings. It is home to the highest rent districts and a thriving financial centre. Expatriates in Seoul can find flats and houses in both regions.

HELP FROM THE ESTATE AGENT

Real estate agents tend to specialise in housing for one specific area. So if you can decide where you wish to live, you will know where to find an estate agent. The English-language newspapers advertise some English-speaking agents; they also specialise. The same agent may cover several apartment complexes and housing types in the same area. Agents for one area may also contact agents from other areas to help you find the type of housing you require.

You can walk into any estate agent's office in the area you have selected, or get references from other expatriates. Any estate agent's office displaying English signs probably speaks some English. The agent will make contact with the owner and take you to the flat or house of your choice.

Once you find a house that you wish to rent, the estate agent will help you agree the contract, and he collects commission from both parties, usually a percentage of the rent. Visit as many estate agents as you like, but only pay the one who took you to the house or flat you eventually decide to rent. If upgrades or repairs need to be made, these need to be clearly spelled out and it is best to have them done before all the rent has been paid. Once the rent is paid, the landlord will feel less urgency to get the changes made.

SYSTEMS FOR PAYING RENT

A few landlords accept rent paid by the month, a method of payment which is convenient for those who might move out of the country with little notice. Most flats and homes rented to expatriates, however, require one or two whole year's rent in advance, which can be quite a fortune.

Koreans have a different system of paying for rent, and some expatriates are able to rent in this way. A large deposit, called 'key money', one third to one half the value of the home, is paid when the contract is made but when you move out, you are refunded the entire amount. In place of rent, the owner of the home or flat collects interest on the large deposit. Some owners ask for a combination of 'key money' and monthly rent: for example, US $10,000 'key money' plus US $2000 a month. The key money will be refunded when you move out, the monthly rent will not.

Appliances and Furniture

It is not customary for landlords to provide appliances though some that rent to expatriates do. One may be able to purchase them for the previous resident or from another expatriate leaving the country and buying new Korean appliances is another option. Homes and flats in Korea are generally equipped for appliances using 220V and 60-hertz. Both the voltage and frequency (hertz) can be different from your home country. Voltage transformers are readily available but frequency conversions are more difficult to make. Consequently, it is probably best to leave your own large appliances at home (refrigerator, stove, washer and dryer). Some flats or homes built for expatriates may have both 110V and 220V.

One can purchase a wide variety of high quality furniture in Korea so buying it here is a good option. However, many people want to have their own furniture so ship it with their household goods.

Utilities And Maintenance

Costs for utilities vary considerably between the different types of housing. Electricity in Korea is more costly than in many other countries. Houses can cost much more to heat and cool than flats, but flats can have high monthly maintenance fees. Monthly electricity, water and telephone bills will come by post and must be paid in person at any bank or post office. Koreans often pay their bills online but this is often only available in the Korean language. Some companies do this for their expatriate employees.

Security

Apartment blocks provide guards to each flat entrance and the cost of guards is included in the monthly maintenance fee. Expatriates living in houses frequently choose to have a home security company provide an alarm system. Though violence towards people is rare in Korea, thievery is common in unoccupied homes.

Maids

It used to be that nearly all expatriates living in Korea employed a maid in the home. As the cost of labour has risen, many expatriates now manage things on their own. Depending on one's living situation and one's financial resources, one may decide to employ a maid to come in to clean once or twice a week. Some expatriate families employ a full time maid and/or nanny. The best way to find a maid is to get one from an expatriate who is leaving the country. Foreigners often try to find their loyal maids new homes before they themselves leave Korea. Get in touch with other expatriates. If no one can refer a maid to you, there are several agencies in larger cities that train their own maids, some of whom can speak your native language and who are familiar with western customs. There are also maid services which allow you to hire someone to do one-time cleaning. Korean maids usually are older women as younger women find other kinds of employment more attractive.

Filipino maids have the advantage of speaking English. However, they will not be able to manage callers at the door or take care of simple tasks which require the use of Korean. So there are advantages and disadvantages to hiring someone who speaks English well at the expense of Korean language proficiency. Plus, not everyone can bring in or hire a maid from another country. Your embassy or Korean immigration can inform you about what your immigration status allows.

Probably even more important than language is whether you feel comfortable with her. This will be evident almost immediately. Does she show you a proper degree of respect? Is she cheerful, talkative, silent, passive, neat and generally to your liking? This person will be in your home, and if you are not comfortable with her, your adjustment to Korea will be much harder.

Interview a maid before you hire her. Check that her language ability is satisfactory. It is very difficult to find one who speaks well, but the more simple directions she understands, the easier it will be for both of you to adjust to each other.

Once you have decided to hire someone, agree on how much you will pay, when you will pay (daily, weekly or monthly) and what bonuses will be paid. Usually one full month's bonus is given at Chusok or New Year (either 1 January or the lunar New Year—*see Chapter Four*), or both. If you are hiring more than one person, make sure they understand who you consider to be the one in charge. Talk about what happens if the maid is sick.

Bathrooms

Koreans use bathrooms differently than westerners. Bathroom floors are rarely dry. When many Koreans bathe at home, they stand on the bathroom floor and spray the shower nozzle over themselves. All Korean bathrooms have a drain in the floor for this purpose. A pair of rubber shoes is kept just outside every bathroom, so that the feet do not get wet whenever one steps inside. A bathroom is usually cleaned by splashing water over the mirror, sink and floor. If you have a rug on a tiled bathroom floor it is likely to get wet if cleaned in the traditional Korean way.

Gardeners

Expatriates may employ gardeners to work for a few days each week. Generally, he will keep any garden in lovely shape without being told what to do. If you have some specific instructions concerning the garden, feel free to say so.

Guards

In Korea, few people would dream of ever leaving their houses unattended. One expatriate stepped outside to pick up some things at a nearby market. Ten minutes later, she discovered her house had been burgled. The police were called and it took them only a minute to discover the culprit—herself! To leave one's house with no-one in it is an open invitation.

A maid can occupy your house in your absence during the day, and even at night if she lives in. But for more protection, some homes employ a night guard. All apartment complexes also retain guards. Their salary is low, and their job not particularly interesting. It is appropriate, therefore, to give them small gifts on Chusok and New Years. This ensures their careful attention in the event that you need it.

Callers At The Door

Answering the door at your home in Korea is a challenge to those expatriates who do not speak Korean and do not have a driver or maid on hand. It is surprising how many salesmen selling books, plant sellers, cosmetics salesgirls, church members and local officials manage to make it to your home. Even if you speak some Korean, you are unlikely to understand exactly what they want.

There is also some danger in answering the door. It is a good way for thieves to briefly scan the inside of your house for valuables, or even force themselves into your home. Many Koreans refuse to open the door for anyone they do not know and it would be wise for you to do the same.

TELECOMMUNICATIONS AND MEDIA
Telephone
Landlords usually provide a telephone connection but you must provide the phone and if you want the landlord to pay for the installation of additional lines, this should be specified in your contract. Expatriates can apply for the installation of a phone line at the local telephone office. A copy of your passport or alien registration card and bank account are required. The cost of a phone service is reasonable but will vary somewhat depending on usage. Calls made to mobile phones are more expensive. Overseas calls are cheapest when made with calling cards, which are readily available on the Internet or at shops throughout Korea.

Korea and Japan are said to be the highest per capita mobile phone users in the world. In fact, Korea was the first country in the world where the number of mobile phone lines exceeded the number of land lines. Virtually everyone in Korea has a mobile phone, and you can expect to be asked for your mobile phone number on a regular basis. The cost of purchasing the phones is high but the monthly service charge is reasonable. Unfortunately, mobile phones from other countries will not work with the mobile phone providers in Korea but it is possible to buy used mobile phones within the country. Note, however, that it is more difficult for expatriates in Korea to subscribe to a mobile phone service than for Korean nationals. If possible, get someone from your company or a Korean friend to get you a mobile phone. Three mobile phone companies exist in Korea: SK Telecom , KTF and LG Telecom. KTF does not require expatriates to make the hefty deposit that the other companies require and pre-paid phone plans are definitely easier to get but do cost more. Mobile phones can easily be rented for short periods at Inchon airport. Charges are reasonable and made by the day.

Public pay phones also exist in Korea. Phone cards for these phones can be purchased many places. However, with almost universal access to mobile phones (many elementary school students have their own mobile phone), many phone booths have been removed so finding them is not always easy. Emergency phone numbers throughout Korea are 112 for police, 119 for fire and ambulance.

INTERNET

Korea is said to have the highest number per capita of Internet connections in the world. One can subscribe to broadband and DSL phone lines for fast connections and wireless Internet connections are also readily available. If you use your phone to connect to the Internet, know that your phone bill is determined by the minutes used so people spending hours on the internet may want to select a phone plan suitable for their Internet use. Well-known Internet service providers include KT Corp, Hanaro Telecom, Ince. Korea Thrunet Co. and Onse Telecom Co. Korean or expatriate contacts can recommend a company suitable for your needs. In addition, you can expect every school and business to have easy access to the Internet and many people use the Internet cafés (called PC Bang) which offer quite reasonable hourly fees throughout Korea. Computers can be purchased within the country or you can bring your own desktop or laptop from home.

Internet access is a lifeline for expatriates. It offers access to your favourite newspapers, radio stations such as BBC or NPR and a whole wealth of information about Korea. Many expatriates, of course, value its ability to keep them in close communication with friends and family back home. Even English teachers posted in rural parts of Korea can have real time, free communication with loved ones over instant-messaging. The Internet can greatly reduce isolation.

Television

Several Korean networks and AFN Korea (American Armed Forces Network) can be viewed free of charge. For more programmes in English, Japanese, Chinese and European languages, expatriates can subscribe to satellite or cable television. Satellite set up is expensive. You may want to ask your landlord to include this in your lease. To subscribe to your service as a foreign resident, you are required to make a large deposit unless a Korean citizen is willing to serve as a guarantor.

Newspapers

Three English-language daily newspapers can be delivered to your home or read online. The Korean Herald (http://www. koreaherald.co.kr), Korea Times (http://www.koreatimes.co.kr) and the International Herald Tribune (http://www.joongangdaily. joins.com).

TRANSPORT
Taxis

Taxis are generally easy to find and an economical way to get around cities. One doesn't have to worry about how to get to one's destination, dealing with ticket machines, bus or underground train stops or parking. General taxis known as *ilban* cost 1,900 won for the first 2 km and an additional 100 won for each 168 m. When the taxi goes slower than 15 km per hour, there is an additional charge of 100 won per 41 seconds. There is also a late night surcharge. Deluxe taxis are larger, black and have the words 'deluxe taxi' or 'jumbo taxi' written on the side of the cab. They cost 4500 won for the first 3 km and 200 won for each additional 205 m. There is a 200 won charge for every 50 seconds when the speed drops below 15 km per hour. Taxi drivers are quite willing to provide extra services too, such as waiting while you pick up something or loading luggage into the trunk. Taxis can be called from mobile phones or from home but there is an additional 1000 won fee for this service. Deluxe taxis in Seoul can be called at (02) 3431 5100. Regular taxis can be reached by calling (02) 1588 0082 or (02) 1588 3382. Unfortunately, the taxi operators are not all able to communicate in English. Since the address system in Seoul is confusing, it is best to give the name of a landmark such as a hotel, post office or apartment complex name and the name of the district. The same information should be given for your destination. Having a map with Korean directions is also helpful.

Catching A Taxi

Taxi's can be hailed along most streets and in specific taxi stands. While taxis are generally easy to find, it is more difficult to catch one during morning or evening rush hour, in the middle of the night and during shift change, which is around 4:00 pm. It is not necessary to be at an intersection or particular place to catch a taxi, however, do not stand in a bus stop to catch a taxi. As u-turns can be difficult to make, it is best to stand on the side of the street according to the direction you are going. Taxi's that are not in use have their top light on and if others are waiting for a taxi, it is polite to let them take the first one that stops—usually others follow this policy. Once you see a vacant taxi, make eye contact with the driver and put your arm out, parallel to the street. Summon the taxi by waving your hand on your extended arm. Raising your arm high and waving your whole arm, as is done in some western countries, is not done in Korea.

Getting To Your Destination

Once the driver stops, get in the back seat on the passenger side (the driver side rear door is always locked). If there are three people, one must sit in the front and that person is required, by law, to wear a seatbelt. The driver will likely begin driving before he has asked where you are going and you can either give the driver a piece of paper with the name and area of your destination or you can say it verbally. It is worthwhile learning to pronounce the name of common destinations clearly or the driver may not understand you. Knowing some Korean phrases, such as "Stop here" or "Go left at the traffic light" is very helpful but expatriates without this knowledge seem to manage to make it to their destination. It is helpful that most taxi drivers have mobile phones and there is a system of volunteer translators that the driver can be connected to. These translators are free and may be invaluable if you and your driver cannot communicate.

Once you reach your stop, pay the driver the cost on the meter. No tip is necessary and drivers are surprised and pleased when expatriates insist that they keep the change.

Sharing A Taxi (Hapseung)

Sometimes when a taxi driver is driving one passenger to a destination he may pick up additional passengers going in the same direction. Each passenger will then pay the full fare for the distance that she or he travelled. This happens particularly during rush hour and has several advantages, notably that more people get rides and the taxi driver can earn extra money. To find additional passengers, the driver will slow down as he passes people waiting for a taxi. They will call out their destination and if the destination is in the direction of the original passenger, the driver will suddenly stop and motion for that rider to get in. If a group of people are riding together, such as you and your spouse, the taxi fare will be the same as one person riding alone. *Hapseung* is illegal and becoming less common with taxi drivers even less likely to practice it with foreign passengers.

City Bus

Buses are a cheap and reliable method of transportation within Seoul and other cities. In some congested parts of the city, bus lanes allow buses to move faster than cars. There are hundreds of bus lines and there is likely one that will take you to your destination. The Seoul bus routes can be found on the Internet but most people become familiar with them by asking others who take the route. In addition, bus drivers, who speak little English, are generally willing to answer questions. A website with route information in English can be found at http://www.lifeinkorea.com/Information/Trans/seoul-trans.cfm#Buses. Specific bus routes for Seoul can be found at http://english.seoul.go.kr/images/SeoulBusMap.pdf.

There are two main types of buses. The first, the IlBan bus, is a regular city bus and the most inexpensive. It is usually bright yellow/orange but sometimes pastel blue and green. These buses have only one seat on each side of the aisle, allowing more passengers to be crammed standing into the bus during rush hour. These buses run so frequently that there is no set schedule—just wait a few minutes and the next bus will arrive. The second type, JwaSeok buses, are more expensive, have two seats on each side of the aisle and do not allow standing. They tend to make fewer stops.

If you are standing and have books or packages, a person sitting near you may pull at your packages, indicating that they will hold them for you. Koreans avoid talking to one another when offering to hold a standing passenger's articles and expatriates unfamiliar with this custom may initially think someone is trying to steal their package.

Bus Payment

It is possible to pay by cash (adult fare is 800 won for the IlBan bus, 1300 won for the JwaSeok bus) but it is much simpler to pay by either a pre-paid transportation card or a debit card issued by a bank. One pays either by cash or card at the front of the bus when one first enters. The bus driver can provide you with change but he and the other passengers don't appreciate the time it takes to do this. Transportation cards can be purchased or re-charged at kiosks near many bus stops. Every time you use the card, the monetary balance will be shown on the meter screen. The same happens when using debit cards but it is more efficient to use the transportation card instead of cash as you will benefit from a small discount. There is also a discount for using a card if one transfers between buses or underground railways. To get the discount one must scan the card again when leaving the bus.

Getting Off The Bus

When taking a new route, it may be difficult to know where to get off the bus. Although many buses are equiped to announce the next stop in Korean and English, it is wise to ask a friend or keep your eyes open for familiar landmarks. You may also tell or show the bus driver where you want to get off. As you approach your stop, push a buzzer that is located along the sides of the bus. Hold it long enough to make the buzzers light up. With IlBan buses, you will need to get off the bus at the back door as quickly as possible.

Underground Railways

The Seoul subway system is clean, convenient and has the advantage of moving quickly despite traffic above. During morning rush hour, it is uncomfortably crowded as everyone goes to work but during other times of the day, you are likely to get a seat. There are 8 colour-coded routes. These routes, with English and Korean labels, are displayed at each stop and on each railways carriage. Pocket-sized route maps are available in English, Japanese and Korean. Busan, Gwangju and Taegu also have efficient underground railways systems and there is also a website in English (http://www.smrt. co.kr/swf/english/cyberstation/main.swf) to help you plan your underground route in Seoul.

Paying For The Underground

There are four methods for paying for the underground. One can purchase a ticket at an underground window or at a ticket dispensing machine. You can buy a pre-paid ticket that can be used until the money on it is used up. These can be purchased at a ticket vending machine or from the attendant at the window for 5000, 10,000 or 20,000 won. Another option is using a pre-paid transportation card and the fourth option is using a credit-based transportation card. These last two options are used for the bus as well. The basic fare is 800 won but if you travel outside certain zones it may go up 100 won. To pass through the turnstile, insert your ticket, go through the turnstile and collect the ticket as it comes out at the turnstile exit. If you are using a card, you pass it over a small screen and wait for it to register. You can then go through the turnstile. If you have a child under

6 travelling with you, keep them close to you as you pass through the turnstile.

Riding The Underground

The signs to find the correct subway and the correct direction are in English and maps are displayed at every choice point but one must pay close attention the first time one is at a specific stop. Getting to some trains may mean going up and down many escalators and walking considerable distance. The same is true when transferring from one train to another. Knowing the colour of the train line you are looking for and the next stop in the direction you are going helps get you on the correct train. When riding escalators, keep right if you plan to stand, allowing those walking up the escalators to pass on the left. Before the train arrives, there is an announcement and at that time people line up at designated places (where the doors will open). Let passengers get off before entering and let seniors and people riding with children to enter first. There are seats for seniors and those with disabilities in some carriages but you can sit there if no one else needs these seats. Mobile phone use is not prohibited on the undergound.

Getting Off The Underground

The underground trains stop at every station. On some lines, the stop is announced in Korean and English. Move close to the exit as your approach the stop you require and get off. Finding your way to another train or to the exit may take the same level of attention as getting on the right train. To exit one must again go through a turnstile. Tickets are re-inserted and cards are swiped again. There are usually many exits at any one underground station and knowing the number of the exit is helpful or you may end up on the wrong side of the street. Maps show the exit numbers which correspond to certain parts of the intersection. If you are visiting a friend, ask which exit number to take and memorise the exit numbers to places you commonly travel to. Otherwise you may emerge from the underground station and realise you need to go down again to get to the right exit.

Automobile

If you are used to driving in your home country you may want the freedom to drive your own car in Korea as many expatriates do. Some companies provide drivers for their foreign employees. Expatriates may pay for their own driver but this is costly. Having a driver has several advantages: one doesn't have to worry about parking, finding out how to get places and a driver can take various people in the family to different destinations throughout the day. Since driving in Korea may be less orderly than that in one's home country and it is done in very tight quarters, some expatriates choose not to drive, at least not at first. It can also take time for expatriates to get used to Korean drivers, which some find to be aggressive. On the toher hand, one can also get along quite well without a vehicle and expatriates who find public transportation convenient also rent a car for the times when they want to travel away from the city in which they live.

If you plan to drive in Korea it is a good idea to get an international driver's licence before arriving. After a few months, you should obtain a Korean licence. Unless your home country recognises the Korean driver's licence, you will have to pass a written exam in Korea to obtain a Korean driver's licence. The exam can be taken in English, Chinese, Japanese and French. An international license must be obtained in one's own country before coming to Korea.

Be Aware

Driving with a license from another country is the same as driving without a licence and an international driver's licence is only valid if the driver is in Korea for less than 90 days. Driving under the influence is strictly prohibited and penalties for driving under the influence are high.

As well as a valid licence, it is also important to have insurance in the event that you are in an accident.

Automobile insurance can be purchased from Korean or international insurance companies but all must be licensed by the Korean government. International companies have the advantage of having the information printed in English and offering more comprehensive coverage but they also are more expensive.

Automobile Costs

Besides the cost of purchasing a vehicle, obtaining a licence, insurance and petrol, owners must also pay a tax every three months. The cost of the tax depends on your automobile make and year and can be paid at banks. After paying the tax you will receive a sticker which must be displayed on your vehicle. Every two years, vehicles less than ten years old must be inspected and you must pay for any required repair costs, which are primarily costs related to pollution emissions.

TRAVELLING WITHIN KOREA

Since Korea is a small country, it is easy to travel around. You have three choices of modes of public transport: airplane, train (three kinds) and express bus. Tickets can be purchased through travel agents, the Internet, by phone and at various ticketing outlets (including some ATM's). The Korean National Tourism Organization has a helpful phone number that provides information for English speaking travellers wanting to travel within Korea. One can dial 1330 in Seoul or 02-1330 from mobile phones, or area code + 1330 from other areas. However, making reservations on the Internet often requires a national citizenship number, making it impossible

Seoul Station, where one can catch trains from Seoul to other cities.

for expatriates to complete a booking this way. It may work but it is best to get assistance from a travel agent or from Korean friends when planning a trip in Korea, particularly if your knowledge of Korean is limited.

WHAT TO BRING FROM HOME

Expatriates in Korea manage quite well with products purchased within the country. The quality and variety of local items is good and they are reasonably priced. The main items you will want to bring to Korea are usually those that are familiar and will make you feel comfortable, as well as those for which you have particular or unique needs. Though there are high quality cosmetics and toiletries available in Korea, you may want to bring your favourite products until you know which ones are available in the country. The one item that expatriates repeatedly report needing to bring is deodorant. Koreans do not have the unpleasant body odour that many westerners have, so deodorant is not commonly used, nor widely available. Some expatriates also bring fluoridated toothpaste and dental floss.

Though most prescriptions can be dispensed in Korea, it may take a while to find a doctor so it would be wise to bring enough to last for 4-6 months. Remember that particular brands of vitamins and supplements may also not be available. Kitchen supplies can easily be bought but many people prefer cooking with their familiar pots and pans so most families bring them from home. It can also be difficult to find a wide variety of clothes, shoes and underwear in larger sizes since Koreans are generally smaller than many westerners. When choosing which clothes to bring, keep in mind that Korean weather tends to the extremes so you'll need warm clothes for the cold winter and cool clothes for the hot summer days. Educational products for children in English or other non-Korean languages are expensive and the variety is limited so you may want to purchase those before you come. If you are bringing a pet and your pet has particular food needs, due to allergies, for example, bring a year's supply of food. High quality cat and dog food is available but the selection is somewhat limited. Veterinarians can care for your pet's health but if your pet takes regular medication, it is best to bring that as well.

EDUCATION

Most expatriates in Korea are satisfied with the education their children receive from pre-school through to secondary school. Finding a curriculum that will prepare one's children for the transition back into schools in their home country is always important. Some families choose a foreign school nearest their home whilst others choose a home in an area close to a school they want their children to attend. In Seoul, schools for expatriate children provide a bus service to many areas of the city.

Education in English is available in Seoul from pre-school age through to college. More limited education is available in German, Chinese, Japanese and French. The cost of this education is quite high and most often paid by one's employer. Since people from the United States have made up a large percentage of the foreign population in Korea, many of the schools for foreigners are geared to children from the United States. However, some families coming from other countries would prefer a more international focus. In addition, many of the schools are faith based and though they welcome children from all faiths, they do include religion as part of their curriculum.

Most foreigners living in Korea send their children to one of the many foreign schools. A few non-Korean families have sent their children to Korean schools, and have been quite satisfied. Expatriate children readily learn the Korean language, and upon returning to western education, find themselves well ahead of their classmates, especially in mathematics and the sciences. They appear to have no particular problem fitting in with their Korean classmates.

Children with special learning needs are not easily accommodated in foreign schools in Korea. It is important for families to explore educational options for their children before making the choice to live in Korea. Home school is an option but only if one parent is available to supervise one of the many home school curriculums.

Sending a child to a Korean school requires much forethought, and while a good decision for some, it is not what most expatriates do. Talking to other expatriates who have made this choice would be a necessary step before embarking on it. *(Refer to the Resource Guide at the back of this book for more information).*

BOOKS

There are an increasing number of books available in English about Korea, with topics as diverse as tourism, Korean cuisine and shamanism. Although most are readily available in Korea, it is worthwhile to get hold of a few before you arrive. If they are not available in your country, write to your Korean employer, and ask them to send what seems to be the most useful from the list in the later chapter of this book called Further Reading.

If you are in Korea, there are several good places to purchase such books. A well-established bookshop in Seoul is the Kyobo Book Centre, in the basement of the Kyobo Building, across from the Sejong Cultural Centre in Kwanghwamun. There is a large selection of books in English on various topics, and a smaller selection in English about Korea. Another favourite shop for English speakers to buy books CD's and DVD's (including Korean movies with English subtitles) is Seoul Selection:

http://www.seoulselection.com/index.html.

HEALTH

Health care in Korea is comparable to other developed countries, though some of the practices are somewhat different. After moving into your home, you should find out the location of the nearest hospital so that in case of emergency, you will know where to go. In Seoul, a 24-hour English speaking emergency medical referral service can be reached at 010-4769-8212 or 010-8750-8212. For less urgent referrals, email medicalreferral@seoul.go.kr.

Korea has no particular health issues. While water is generally assumed to be safe to drink, Koreans and expatriates usually have bottled water delivered to their home. Bottled water can also be purchased easily throughout the country.

Doctors And Hospitals

Many Korean doctors have some knowledge of English, and those who have studied abroad are quite fluent in English, Japanese or German. There are many very well qualified doctors, and medical care in Korea is of high quality. Nevertheless, getting healthcare in a foreign country is anxiety-provoking. One of the best ways of finding care is by word-of-mouth recommendations from friends. Another option is to contact the international clinic closest to where you live.

When Koreans go to the doctor, they generally do not expect medical explanations for their problems, instead trusting the doctor to decide what medical care they need. Korean doctors accustomed to working with western patients understand that these patients are likely to want a specific diagnosis, to ask numerous questions and may want an active role in making medical decisions. Nevertheless, to communicate the details of a patient's medical condition is not usual and some expatriates become frustrated with these cultural differences in health communication. Gently but firmly asking for information works best. Seeking referrals to a doctor you can communicate well with is another option.

Most hospitals in Korea have outpatient offices on the ground floor, so if you go to a large hospital you can probably get outpatient care for some medical problems. When your Korean friend says he needs to go to the hospital, he is probably referring to the outpatient offices, not the emergency room.

There are also numerous private clinics, often within walking distance of residential areas. Usually the clinic sign is written in English, often accompanied by a green cross-the symbol for medical care. Commonly, visits to these involve no waiting time, and the care is more personal than in hospitals, although the range of services can, of course, be limited. While doctors at most clinics usually have some command of English, the staff can rarely communicate well in this language.

In-patient hospital care in Korea is different than that in many western hospitals. Family members generally provide most of the physical care, including meals, and someone should stay with the patient around the clock. This is beginning to change in Korea, with nurses providing more care but probably still not at the level you might receive in your home country. There will also, of course, be significant communication problems if you do not speak Korean.

Chemists

There are several *yak bang* (chemists) located in every neighbourhood. To communicate accurately, it is best to have the prescription written on paper, in either English or Korean. Prescriptions are also available at international clinics. High quality Korean and imported medication is readily available and some doctors will give their patients medication directly, without telling them what it is. If you have mediation which you take on a regular basis, it is wise to bring several months worth with you to give you time to find a doctor and chemist in your area.

Dentists

The quality of dental care in Korea is quite good and orthodontic care is also available. Dental clinics are easy to find in any large city in Korea and the equipment and procedures are comparable to those in western countries. Referrals can be obrained from other expatriate or Korean friends.

Health Insurance

Some expatriates have health insurance from home that covers some or all of their medical costs while in Korea. It is possible for companies or individuals to purchase Korean national health insurance for expatriate residents of Korea. An application can be downloaded at www. nhic.or.kr. Foreigners who have used this are generally quite satisfied with it and surprised how reasonably priced it is.

Bathrooms

Not so long ago, public bathrooms in Korea were one of the aspects of Korean life that expatriates complained about the most. Fortunately, this is no longer the case. Public restrooms are usually easy to find, generally clean and are stocked with tissue paper. In large public restrooms, the toilet paper may be located on one large roll outside the stalls so be sure to check before you go into the stall and it wouldn't hurt to carry your own tissue just in case. Traditional toilet basins are stood over, not sat on and it is possible still possible to find these old style bathrooms today.

Eye Care

There are many high quality eye clinics located throughout Korea. One can have vision tests at these clinics and order glasses or contact lenses. Eye prescriptions from home can also be easily dispensed for a reasonable price.

MONEY

Until recently, Korea was a cash economy and expatriates who have become accustomed to using credit cards and debit cards may find their way of paying for things in Korea is different, particularly if you are living outside a major city.

The unit of Korean currency is won. Coin denominations are W5, W10, W50 and W500. Bank notes are issued in W1000, W5000 and W10,000. They are each a different colour so it is easy to tell them apart. Bank cheques are drawn for W100,000 and over.

Foreign currency and Korean cheques can be converted into Korean won at foreign exchange banks and other authorised moneychangers. The international airport in Inchon can exchange money, either cash or traveller's cheques, upon arrival. Be aware that ATM's are not a good way to convert foreign money into Korean won.

Banks

Foreigners can open a bank account at most Korean banks and at many foreign bank branches. Bring a passport and/or an Alien Registration Certificate to the bank when opening an account. The use of ATM's is expanding, but some expatriates find they cannot do as much in English at Korean ATM's as they could in their home country. ATMs are generally located inside the banks, usually in a separate section to the side, and can be accessed from 8:00 a.m. to 10:00 p.m. They are used widely by Koreans to pay utility bills and make transfers; however, the menu options for English speaking users may be fewer. Most ATM's allow only for foreigners to make deposits, withdrawals and transfers. These cash points can be found at major hotels, department stores, underground train stations and tourist spots with internationally recognised ATM cards widely accepted. Koreans have embraced online banking and this service is also available to expatriates in English. If you want to withdraw money from your Korean bank account when abroad you will need to request a special ATM card for this purpose from your Korean bank.

While personal cheques are virtually unheard of in Korea, it is useful to have a chequeing account in your home country. This allows you to transfer money to and from Korea and to pay bills by cheque in your home currency. Credit cards, both foreign and Korean, are accepted at department stores, some restaurants and an increasing number of other places. Since Korean credit cards for foreigners are costly, many expatriates use their credit cards from home but they then must be paid for in one's home currency. Credits cards are becoming more widespread but some foreign cards are not accepted at particular shops.

Tax

Value-added tax (VAT) is charged on most goods and services at a standard rate of ten per cent and is included in the retail price. Hotels charge ten per cent tax to rooms, meals and other services. This is added to the bill. Information on income tax for expatriates living in Seoul can be found at http://www.kexpat.com/tax5.htm and http://www.metro.seoul.kr/eng/living/index_tax.html.

SHOPPING

Expatriates living in Seoul have many shopping options. Those living outside of Seoul used to make regular trips to the city to stock up on products but now most products which are considered important to westerners can be found in other cities as well.

Supermarkets

Modern, clean supermarkets scattered throughout Korea meet the needs of most expatriates as Koreans eat many western style foods, including breakfast cereal, baby food, frozen pizza, cheese, convenience foods and bakery goods. For more specialised western or other foreign foods, there are particular supermarkets which cater to various expatriate tastes. At supermarkets, prices are fixed and clearly marked. Outside, you can find black market sellers who will take special orders for particular brands and items not available inside the shop.

Outdoor Markets and Small Neighbourhood Shops

Near most neighbourhoods are often outdoor markets which offer fresher and usually cheaper foods and other items. There are other small markets, indoor and outdoor, that sell everything from silk and custom-made clothes to door knobs, fresh fish and vegetables. Buying from markets is less

Southgate Market in Seoul.

convenient as one must bargain and purchase each item separately. Most neighbourhoods also have small, individually owned shops which are not part of a chain and thse may accept bargaining. Convenience shops which are part of a chain have fixed prices.

Traditional Korean Markets

Many expatriates find that going to large Korean markets is one of their favourite activities. Your first visit to one of these larger markets may be overwhelming as you may get pushed around a bit but the sights, smells and sounds that you experience will stay with you long after you leave Korea. Merchandise at these places does not seem to be arranged in any organised fashion, and food may not be as sanitary as you might wish. There is no room for cars, so all your wandering will be on foot. As there are also no shopping carts, it would be wise to take a comfortable shopping bag when embarking on such an adventure.

Bargaining

Smaller, individually owned shops and booths generally expect shoppers to bargain. Bargaining is becoming less common in Korea compared to years ago and the amount one can save by bargaining is generally less than half the first price offered.

When you bargain, the first thing to do is to express modest interest in the article. Look it over critically for flaws. Then ask the price. The seller will always tell you a price higher than the one he or she is willing to accept, because by lowering it, you will appear to have been given a favour.

Offer to pay somewhere between half and 75 per cent of the first price. Korean buyers are careful to study the reaction of the seller to their counter offer. If the seller is not shocked, they advise, you should lower your offer. In any case, you will probably be told that your offer is below cost, then be given another offer, somewhere in the region of between your offer and the seller's. You can take it if it seems reasonable, or continue bargaining. Or you can walk away. The seller may take your highest offer as you leave.

It is sensible to look around at various shops or booths to get a general idea of how much a particular item costs. This puts you in a better position to bargain. However, if you have allowed a shopkeeper to go to a great deal of trouble to find what you want, you should not leave without buying something. This is especially true if the shopkeeper has gone to another shop to obtain the item you requested, as is frequently done.

Many expatriates who speak Korean are angered when they discover that they have been asked to pay up to three times as much as a Korean customer at the same booth. The seller reasons that, being a foreigner, you can afford to pay the higher price. However, if it means losing a sale, the seller will give you, too, that lower price.

Superstition always surrounds the first interaction of the day. If the first shopper walks away from a purchase, bad luck is supposed to stay with the seller all day. For this reason, if you are shopping early in the day, you may get a very good price but if you walk away, the owner may appear unreasonably upset.

Large Retailers

Korea now has a variety of large retailers from other countries including Carrefor Korea, Costco, Walmart and Homeplus (TESCO) which offer a huge variety of reasonably priced items. Korean department stores, including Shinsegae, Midopa and Lotte, offer very high quality goods and the excellent service and high prices that one would expect. Gourmet grocery shops and tasty restaurants aimed at wealthy Koreans are housed in the basements of each of these. Organic food is not widely available but can be found and it is not surprising that such food would appeal to health-conscious Koreans.

Rubbish And Recycling

Koreans are required to adhere to a strict recycling plan. Rubbish/recyling collection is paid for by purchasing rubbish bags. White bags, which are used for residential recycling, can be purchased in 50, 70 and 100 litre sizes at most local grocery shops. Each area has its own type on type of bag so be sure to purchase your recycling bags in the area that you live.

CULTURAL ADJUSTMENT

While settling into one's new living environment is a complex and difficult task, it is not the only adjustment that one will have to make when moving to Korea. Everyone moving to a new country experiences something called 'Culture Shock'—even people who have lived abroad before. Culture shock has been defined as a special kind of anxiety and stress experienced by people who enter a culture radically different from their own. Suddenly, the methods one has always used to accomplish particular tasks are not effective. Culture shock is generally experienced during the first six months to a year after entering a new culture and few people escape this particularly stressful period, regardless of how positive they felt initially about entering the new culture.

What Is Culture Shock?

- Culture shock refers to the unique problems people have while they are adjusting to a new culture.

A fashionable shopping district near Yonsei University.

- Culture shock is a psychological situation where one no longer feels in control.
- Culture shock includes two kinds of problems: being confused, anxious and puzzled by the way others behave; and confusion, causing anxiety to, and puzzling others by behaving in one's own way.
- Culture shock originates from the belief that everyone is the same.

Upon entering a new culture, a person does not know how to behave. Newcomers to Korea do not know when to bow, or how to pour alcohol for an older person. They do not know how to criticise an employee or how to dress for a special occasion. They do not know how to buy something at the market, or what to do when someone hands you an empty glass. These are among the thousands of instances of cultural behaviour that all Koreans automatically know. Newcomers cannot expect to learn the Korean ways of thinking and behaving in a few weeks or months.

The Logistical Adjustment

Before exploring the phenomenon of culture shock in greater depth, it is helpful first to recognise the things that are going on in newcomers' lives that make existence difficult, even without culture shock. An expatriate arriving in Korea is addressing innumerable complex issues simultaneously. While one is learning the geography of the city, beginning to get a glimpse of office politics, trying to form new relationships, enrolling children in school, getting a residence not only selected and leased but re-papered, carpeted and furnished, one's body is adjusting to a new climate. While one is figuring out how (or if) to hire a maid, get a driver's licence and how to file a lost luggage claim, one is also grieving the loss of a familiar community, friends, favourite restaurants and a comfortable routine. These changes are difficult, even for seasoned movers. But each of these adjustments could be multiplied by ten when every detail must be negotiated under a different set of cultural rules.

With all these adjustments taking place simultaneously, one does well just to survive. Making a contribution to the job, learning about the country, pursuing meaningful activities, participating in rewarding friendships or learning the language, expectations that one had when one decided to relocate to Korea prove impossible, and yet these expectations did not seem unrealistic at the time.

What may seem like culture shock at first is perhaps more accurately labelled 'moving-to-a-new-country shock'. The real bolt of culture shock current comes only after one has completed some of the practical adjustments; has a roof over one's head, has learned how to get across the city to work and has stocked one's pantry. No doubt this early phase is draining, frustrating and overwhelming and whilst one has certainly had opportunities to interface with the new culture, it is not culture shock per se.

Real culture shock sets in when one has settled in for the long haul. Having adapted more or less to the physical circumstances, one is now in a position to adapt to the cultural circumstances, that is, how Korean people see the world and how they behave, and, perhaps even more to the point, how you see the world and how you will behave in a new cultural environment.

The Unconscious Expectation

Most people moving to Korea have had opportunities to interact with people from other cultures, and know that people's habits and modes of thinking differ. Few people consciously expect everyone to be the same. And yet, when examined carefully, most do operate under the assumption that we are all the same. When movers struggle to remove their shoes as they carry in a sofa, you may think something is wrong with them because they don't behave in the same way as yourself. When asked to sing solo at a social gathering, you may be uncomfortable and perhaps even angry because such a custom is embarrassing in your own culture. These ways of being, thinking and behaving are only surprising, anxiety-provoking and confusing because we all unconsciously hold an expectation that others think, feel and act the same as we do. We prefer an advance invitation; why don't they? We're not offended if people wear shoes in our homes; why are they?

The assumption that under normal circumstances all people think and perceive the world in the same way is necessary to carry out our daily lives. If we couldn't expect people to return our handshakes, stop at red lights, recognise our academic degrees, understand what we meant by a gift and thousands of other things we do or see on a daily basis, we could not organise our lives. These expectations, that are so vital to functioning in our own culture, are the basis of culture shock, and at the root of the numerous symptoms which accompany culture shock.

When Culture Shock Sets In

Culture shock is a pervasive sense of anxiety, confusion, helplessness, irritation and lack of control resulting from a relocation to a different culture, where the expectations we have of others are not being met. There are a number of symptoms, and most people suffer from several simultaneously. Some symptoms stubbornly remain until you are not only adjusted to the culture, but have come to a new self-identity within that culture. Other symptoms, thankfully, crop up only during particularly difficult times, such as when your overseas boss is making an appearance or when a special holiday occurs. It is important to remember that these reactions are normal reactions to an abnormal situation (most people never live outside their own cultures), and that expecting them will make their intrusion upon your life somewhat easier to tolerate.

Excessive Concern Over Cleanliness

Every country has different standards of cleanliness. Koreans are reluctant to eat anything with their fingers and neither would they dream of wearing shoes inside a home. Newcomers, howeverr, do not often notice these manifestations of Koreans' extreme concern over cleanliness issues.

On the other hand, newcomers are often alarmed at the instances where the comparison between Korean and western standards tilts in favour of hygienic western practices. Owners of small Korean restaurants may wash their dishes with cold water. Public bathrooms are not always as clean as a westerner might like. In time, most expatriates learn to overlook such differences, but the newcomer may exaggerate their importance. Some newcomers experiencing culture shock refuse to eat in any Korean restaurant. They may make frequent trips to the doctor, convinced they have contracted an unusual disease.

Feelings of Helplessness and Withdrawal

Expatriates often feel they do not know how to do anything: where to buy mushrooms; how to ride an underground train, how to find out if a business partner understands what they are saying. During culture shock, all annoyances, big or small, become overwhelming. One might try to escape from everything Korean and try to surround oneself with familiar things and people from home. Of course, avoiding the culture completely is impossible, but for a person who wants to withdraw, those inevitable contacts with Korea can be unusually stressful.

False Expectations

Expatriates living in Korea find that they are not the only one's who hold false expectations of others: Koreans may both expect foreigners to behave in ways similar to them and expect all foreigners to be alike. For example, it is hard for Koreans to understand foreigners who prefer to do things alone, as Koreans nearly always enjoy being with others. Many Koreans hold narrow stereotypes of foreigners and when you think or act outside of that, Koreans may have difficulty accepting your individuality.

Depression

Some newcomers go through periods of depression. 'How can I ever adjust to orange kitchen cupboards?' 'What's the use in trying to be happy in my miserable situation?' Along with the depression comes an inability to do anything to improve the situation. Suggestions from family or friends all seem hopeless. In some extreme cases, culture shock has led to clinical depression. There is English speaking professional help available if necessary.

Desire for Home and Friends

The need for friends and family is especially acute. People need their own feelings and reactions validated. Some spend all day online communicating with people back home. Others feel a vacuum that they have never experienced during previous extended separations from family and friends. Some expatriates develop special worries about particular people in their home country, becoming irrationally afraid that their absence will cause loved ones back home unnecessary pain or inconvenience.

Anxiety, Frustrations and Paranoia

Perhaps no expatriate in Korea is able to avoid these symptoms completely. Small frustrations become unconquerable mountains. Some people feel a constant fear that something terrible will happen. Many feel that Koreans are intentionally causing them problems. Some new arrivals believe everyone is trying to cheat them, perhaps even harm them.

Irritability

With so many unknowns and frustrations, it is natural that a person experiencing culture shock should readily feel irritated. Every day is filled with situations where one does not know how to act. It irritates one that simple tasks seem impossible to execute. And one becomes particularly sensitive to small irritations when difficulties pile up.

Obstacles that were brushed off in a familiar environment cannot be so easily forgotten in Korea. Deliveries did not always arrive on time at home, for example, but that was never quite so irritating.

Physiological Stress Reactions

There is a close connection between one's emotional and physical states. People who are experiencing the frustrations and anxiety of culture shock are often more prone to physical problems than other people.

Many newcomers complain that it takes a long time to get used to the water or food in Korea. And, for some, it does. Emotional stress also brings on allergies, back problems, headaches and digestive problems. Fortunately, they go away as soon as the most intense period of culture shock has passed.

Food Challenges

People living in homestays and others eating mostly Korean food find that food is often one of their biggest challenges in the early months in Korea. This can be true even for people who know and like Korean food and for people who have lived in Korea before. Food is central to everyone's life and to suddenly stop eating those foods one holds dear and to be eating food that is notably different can be a shock to one's system. It also is a constant reminder that one is truly living a different life. Korean food is distinct and expatriates find there is a limit to how much garlic, hot pepper, vegetables, fish and rice one can eat. It is worth seeking out familiar foods and to give yourself permission to back away from an exclusive Korean diet.

A Natural Reaction to Culture Shock

The instinctive way to respond to those situations which cause one to feel helpless, irritated, embarrassed and/or anxious is to withdraw from the situation. When bargaining in a different language is too difficult, it is understandable that one might start using mail-order catalogues from home and forgo the market altogether. When asked to attend yet another drinking party where people pour for one another but never for themselves in a perplexing order, it is tempting to stay at home.

It is possible to learn to avoid as many of the unpleasant situations as possible, surrounding oneself with reminders of home, and people who think and behave in familiar ways. Many cling to the expatriate community in Seoul and fill their lives with events which approximate those in their own countries. Much of the time spent in the expatriate community can be spent criticising the host culture and dreaming about the next trip back home. Such conversations validate one's feelings, but they also tend to solidify one's negative opinions about Korea. And although retreating into familiar territory is protection from the irritation and helplessness an expatriate is liable to feel in Korea, it begins a pattern of withdrawing which becomes a spiral of retreat. This prevents one from continuing to have experiences which lead to better knowledge and ultimate cultural adjustment.

A tourist can experience the exotic aspects of a foreign culture, become frustrated when people don't behave as expected, and leave, taking with him souvenirs of Korean celadon, antique chests with brass fixtures, stories of the frustrations with immigration and one's driver. And longer-term residents can live much the same, interacting very little with Korean people, and understanding very little about how ancient Confucian customs affect current marriages or what dreams a young adolescent girl in Korea may have. But by following one's natural reaction to withdraw from experiences which set off culture shock, one is precluded from really understanding that people think and behave in different ways.

An Alternative Reaction to Culture Shock

How then does one avoid the cycle of experiencing unpleasant interactions in Korea, which lead to a withdrawal, which leads to less understanding, which leads in turn to more withdrawal, irritation and increasing frustration?

Since one's expectations that people will act and think like oneself will regularly be unfulfilled, it is not possible to avoid culture shock and its attendant symptoms. But it is possible to view these situations from a different perspective that will contribute to a better understanding of Korean expectations and ultimately to greater comfort and knowledge.

Firstly, it is important to keep in mind that it generally is not the actions per se, but our own unfulfilled expectations that bother us. Singing in the shower or along with the car radio isn't threatening to us, but doing that same action in the company of colleagues is. A cancelled class does not upset most people, but when you are not informed in advance of its cancellation (as would happen in most western countries) it is upsetting. A stranger (albeit a doctor) touching your child's head is not upsetting whereas when it is a person in the market touching your child, it is.

Secondly, when feelings of disgust, agitation or anxiety arise, you need to stand back for a moment and consider why you are experiencing those emotions. Realise that it is because something we had expected to happen does not, or because something we had not expected to happen does. What is bothersome is not what someone else has done (asked you to sing, cancelled a class or touched your child's head), but our expectations that we should not have to sing, should know about cancellations or have our child touched only by a licensed person. When one is able to analyse the source of the feeling (one's own expectations), those feelings generally dissipate.

Thirdly, you need to believe that the anxiety that comes from not knowing what to do in the numerous situations you find yourself in every day is a natural part of learning about Korea, about your own expectations and about yourself. Such anxiety will only diminish by going to the market without a translator, having dinner at a Korean friend's home and negotiating a contract, Korean-style. Think of these early anxiety-provoking situations as a necessary vaccination against future anxieties!

Fourthly, avoid concentrating on the negative emotions such as aggravation, confusion, helplessness and embarrassment, for if you do, you will be prevented from seeing other aspects of the situation and thus gaining knowledge that will be useful for the next related experience. Also, by concentrating on the unpleasantness, you will build up negative expectations with which to view similar experiences in the future.

Having done the above, there will certainly be types of behaviour that, though we can learn to expect, we do not like. For example, though we understand that drinking is a custom with a long tradition in Korea, and that the paid women who may laugh or sing with married men have no intentions of disrupting a marriage, we may still dislike the custom. We may have observed countless such occasions, gained a good deal of knowledge about the custom and become no longer offended by it, but we still cannot accept

This traditional farmers dance that is performed in most outdoor festivals is one of the many examples of the depth and beauty in this East Asian nation.

it for ourselves. This is as it should be. To respect yourself it will be necessary to reject certain aspects of Korea. But those instances will be rare once you have a deep understanding of Korea through personal experience.

MANAGING CULTURE SHOCK

Recognising that culture shock is a normal reaction to an abnormal situation, which arises out of your own expectation that people are all the same, is helpful in diminishing the sting of culture shock. Important, too, is acknowledging your feelings of frustration, instead of letting them prevent you from making observations about the situation. There are other things that you may do as well.

Read About Korea Before You Arrive

If you have time, it is much better to come to Korea with some knowledge about the country that will be your new home. The more you understand about Korea, the better prepared you will be when you arrive. The information in this book is a good start in helping you understand Korean customs and culture. If you are interested in art, history, dance, antiques or Korean cuisine, some reading about those particular topics will give you something to look forward to in your new country.

Meet Other Expatriates

Many close friendships have been made while sitting in a Starbucks coffee house. Just because two people are expatriates: they have something important in common. It seems that once in a foreign country, an expatriate can feel quite comfortable with almost any other foreigner, even those quite unlike friends back home. In Korea, most differences in education, age, economic level or even personality seem minor compared to the similarities of being expatriates.

If you are new, longer-staying expatriates can identify with your difficulties easily. All of them have stories of the problems they had when they first came to Korea, and they are eager to share their store of knowledge as well as suggestions to make your adjustment easier. Experienced expatriates can save newcomers untold hassles.

Some expatriates tell of not seeing a single foreigner for their first six months in Korea. That may be an overstatement, unless one resides in a small village in the country, but it is true that some foreigners do not know how to make contact with other expatriates. It does not need to be very difficult.

If the children go to a foreign school, it is easy to meet other parents at the school. There are business organisations for expatriate business people, and many organisations for women. Within these larger organisations are many special interest groups. There are several churches in languages other than Korean, and some of the Korean adoption agencies have volunteer activities for expatriates.

When meeting other expatriates, it is natural to complain about things which may not be available or reminisce about life back home. Be wary of friends who isolate themselves in the cocoon of the expatriate community and use these friendships to support their withdrawal from Korea. Frustrations need to be validated but too much criticism of the host culture can facilitate negative expectations and prevent one from really understanding the deeper cultural meanings behind stressful interactions.

Re-create Your Own World

While it will certainly be impossible to make living arrangements identical to what you had back home, make an effort to personalise your living space. Put up pictures, use familiar bedspreads, and make sure you have got your favourite frying pan. When so much of your environment is foreign, any familiar article gives comfort.

Make a noticeboard with updated pictures of friends and family. Take advantage of the inexpensive flowers, and make up a bouquet of your favourite variety. If you have children, be sure to bring their own stuffed animals to make their rooms feel familiar. Bring tapes of your favourite music, to listen to when you want to hear the sounds of home. And do not forget your favourite books. DVD's from your home country can be and familiar and comfortable escape when you are overwhelmed with unfamiliar things.

These small steps may seem insignificant, but they really do make your somewhat different-looking home a place to feel at ease. With all the exotic and unusual things that confront you outside, you need a haven of comfort for a retreat.

But as one begins to understand Korea better, Korean objects will almost unconsciously become part of your home, soon to be treasured possessions just as your experience in Korea becomes a part of who you are.

Meet Koreans Of A Similar Social Level

One of the best ways to understand Korea, and to begin the process of enjoying the culture, is through Korean friends. These friends can explain what you do not understand about the country, show you around, and counteract any negative encounters you have had with other Koreans. Your maid, the fruit-seller and the shopkeeper in Itaewon are not the right people. Since Koreans rarely have friendships with people who are not their social equals, you will probably be most satisfied with Korean friends with a background similar to yours. Meeting such friends requires a special effort on your part.

They can most easily be found at some of the same places you meet expatriate friends: international schools, churches and social organisations. Koreans who have lived abroad and wish to keep contact with foreigners are likely to appear there. They are also probably eager to help you get along in Korea, especially having experienced the difficulties of living in a foreign culture themselves.

Learn The Korean Language

This is a rather obvious suggestion, but do not overlook it. Korean is a difficult language for most non-Koreans to learn. Even people who study full-time for a year cannot speak the language fluently. Since many Koreans at tourist attractions and at stores catering to foreigners can communicate sufficiently in English, you may think you can get along well without any language ability. It is still worthwhile, however, to spend as much time as you can studying the language. When Koreans hear you use even a little Korean, they feel that you value their country and language and will warm up to you quickly.

If you learn some basic Korean, for example the numbers and a few questions about prices and bargaining, you can survive well in the market. To get a Korean to understand you in a language so different from your own will give you a sense of satisfaction. You will not feel so alienated when some Korean words start to sound familiar, even if you cannot understand exactly what is said.

Language classes are also a good place to meet other newcomers. No matter what the age, nationality or economic level, the students usually feel a special kinship in their common endeavor to master an exotic language.

Do Not Expect Too Much Of Yourself

Adjusting to a new climate, new food, a new home and new friends, to say nothing of the new culture, is not easy. Newcomers cannot expect to arrive one day and be settled in a week later. Opening a new bank account will not be as simple as it was back home. You cannot expect to order things for your home as painlessly as you did in your own country. Some things you want or need may not exist here. Others take much longer to locate or to be made. Koreans do not understand your strange taste, and they may be surprised when you will not accept a sofa that is 'almost' like the one you ordered (bright red instead of tan).

Jet lag can take more than a week to overcome. The new diet can be difficult to assimilate. Most newcomers find that just living in a new culture tires them, as so many new stimuli bombard the senses. Your body needs time to settle in. Do not expect it to go full steam. Even long-term expatriates find that they seem never to regain the energy they had in their own country. Being regarded as strange by everyone else, trying to understand Korean thinking and behaviour, and worrying that you are always doing something wrong may make you chronically tired.

It is important to recognise that culture shock will take its physical toll on you. Do not blame yourself when you are not as efficient or energetic as you were back home.

Lower Your Expectations Of Others

Just as you yourself will not perform at peak level, your spouse and children will also have difficulties settling in. Culture shock affects everyone. They may do things that were not acceptable back home. Try to understand them and relax some of your expectations. If your children want to stay up and talk past their normal bedtime, do not let it bother you. If your spouse is not quite as tidy as he or she used to be, hold your breath. After an initial adjustment period, many things will return to normal.

The same applies to Koreans who provide services for you. Though you may be quite specific in your instructions, you will often find that things do not get done exactly as you had requested. Your secretary may not understand that when you said 'urgent', you meant 'now'. The people who custom-made your bed might have thought 'king size' and 'double' were the same. Try to relax and be patient. The language and cultural gap between you and them is at its biggest at first. It may take you a while to learn how to make yourself understood.

Consciously Pursue Special Interests

There are hundreds of interests to explore in Korea. By focusing on those things you like and can do, your dissatisfaction with the things you cannot do in Korea will be minimised. All kinds of art classes are available, from calligraphy to water colours to ceramics. Some are not taught in English, but in such classes, language fluency is not always necessary. Any interest in sightseeing or photography can be pursued in depth. You will have opportunities to see things you have never seen in your home country.

People interested in the performing arts will never be bored. World-renowned orchestras, ballet companies and drama groups make their way to Seoul every year. And Korea has her own unique and fascinating dance groups and play companies. Most of these are listed in the English language newspapers.

Sports fans of all kinds have settled quite happily into Korean life. Tennis, golf, volleyball, soccer, hiking, martial arts, swimming, scuba diving, skiing, boating and camping can all be enjoyed in Korea. Some expatriates find they can devote more time to such sports in Korea than they could in their native country.

Connoisseurs of ethnic food will have many opportunities to develop their interests as well. Of course Korean foods of all kinds are widely available, as well as Japanese and Chinese foods. Hotels often import chefs from western countries to prepare a special menu for a week or month. All kinds of superb foods are offered at different times throughout the year. Seoul International Women's Association offers a variety of classes in ethnic cooking.

By becoming involved in activities, an expatriate can begin to appreciate living in Korea. It is easier for those in Seoul to find activities of interest, but expatriates living in outlying areas are rarely far from a major city, where they, too, can find something to enrich their lives.

Recognise that Culture Shock Relapses Often Occur

After you have organised your office and home, become a part of various organisations, found ways to pursue meaningful activities, learned how to get around your Korean city satisfactorily and even come to appreciate many of the unique elements in Korean society as well as in individual Korean friends, there will still be times when all that learning seems for naught, when nothing makes sense any more and when all you can think about is being back where people do things the 'right' way. Will this mean that what you had thought was cultural adjustment was really just a short-term adaptation? Thankfully, the answer to that question is often no.

There will be times when an unfulfilled expectation will catch you off guard and your reaction to it will again be one of anxiety or aversion. Even long-term residents of Korea continue to encounter new situations daily, many of them puzzling and the source of confusion and irritation. Perhaps your secretary will laugh after losing the text for a forthcoming speech, or someone pushes their way in front of you just as you reach the head of the supermarket line. Such an incident may trigger a number of uncomplimentary thoughts about your host country, usually thoughts beginning with 'Why do they...?'

Your frustration is natural and predictable. And you'll need to address it in the same way you dealt with it earlier in your adjustment, by realising the source of your stress is coming from your assumption that everyone thinks, feels and behaves as you do. Instead of condemning the incident which makes you feel apprehensive and bothered, among other things, observe the situation and label the cause of those feelings. Express your frustration to a confidant without assigning blame to the secretary or energetic customer, for it is your expectations, not their actions, which are responsible for your misery. And remember that it is just such experiences that are giving you a new understanding of yourself, your own culture and even Korea, a country so different from your own, but one in which you will learn not only to survive, but to thrive.

PARTICULAR ADJUSTMENT CHALLENGES FOR PARTICULAR PEOPLE

Everyone experiences culture shock in different ways, but particular problems and obstacles attributed to culture shock are likely to occur among specific groups of expatriate people.

Business People

Expatriates doing business or residing in Korea will find themselves spending an inordinate amount of time at work, partly in order to learn a new job and the Korean ways of doing things. Another part of it is the socialisation demanded of all business people in Korea, who have little time for themselves. Yet spending time with the family, and having a break from the stress of business in a new culture, is particularly important while one is adjusting to a new culture.

The Non-Working Partner

While the employed person is overwhelmed with his or her responsibilities at work, the partner is left to cope with settling in the family. A company will often help a foreign employee adjust to his or her new position, but the spouse must figure things out alone. The spouse is also the one who has direct and frequent contact with Koreans—the real estate agent, curtain maker, market vendors and numerous other service people. Each encounter is fraught with difficulties arising from the differences in speed and quality of service between one's home country and Korea.

Many partners coming to Korea are giving up or postponing a career. Adjustment from working outside to working inside a home is never easy, especially when you are in a foreign country and have no ready built social support system. Some partners appreciate the opportunity to have more time to be involved in their children's lives. Others look for unique ways to further their career. For example, one may use this time to learn particular skills, perhaps preparing oneself for a career change. There may be opportunities to do consulting work for Korean or foreign companies or you may be able to learn particular skills through volunteer work with businesses, cultural organisations, schools, churches or social service agencies. Other spouses use this time to focus on hobbies one has long neglected. This time in Korea does not have to be wasted time.

For couples that have long been dual-career, the balance of the relationship will naturally change when one has heavy career demands and the other is left to manage the home. Couples need to talk about these changes and the special challenges each one is facing, recognising the things each are gaining and each or giving up as a result of this new arrangement. Couples need to continue to have time together, for talking and for having fun. If partners seem to be growing apart, counselling is appropriate.

Non-working partners who have not been at home before may be wary of the idea of becoming involved in expatriate clubs. At home these groups may have been for wives of wealthy people who enjoy putting on teas. When expatriates actually go to some of the many events going on in Seoul, they are surprised to meet others who were equally hesitant to participate. The expatriate community is Seoul is extremely active and few people will not find a niche once they meet others and find out about the many possible arenas for involvement. Some of the larger organisational meetings are overwhelming but they are a good way to meet kindred spirits.

Single People

People who have come to Korea with a spouse and/or children are cushioned against some of the frustrations of culture shock. They can at least talk about their difficulties with someone who understands and cares. Single people have no such support system.

Singles do, however, have good opportunities to get to know Koreans and other expatriates. Koreans are very sympathetic towards people who are alone, and they are particularly eager to act as a guide, and to spend time with a foreigner. Other single expatriates are also quite supportive of those in a similar situation.

Some single expatriate women in Korea have found difficulty making close friends. There are far fewer expatriate women in Korea with whom to associate. While expatriate men can easily drink with Korean men, Korean women are not as accessible for friendship with expatriate women, and Korean men are not as accustomed to platonic relationships with women. Foreign women in Korea often find that it is difficult to find men to date, either foreign or Korean.

For single men there are many chances in Korea for interaction with the opposite sex. There are people eager to learn about foreign people of the opposite gender, some even inclined towards a serious relationship with one. Websites and matchmaking services exist to connect you with Korean women open to a relationships with a foreign man.

Another situation that most single expatriates run into often is related to their being unattached. Many Koreans assume that if a person is at or over the marriageable age, he or she is eager to marry. It is difficult to understand how a 35-year-old woman could be satisfied in an unmarried state. It is quite possible that single expatriates of both sexes will be introduced to potential marriage partners by well-meaning colleagues and friends. For some, this will be fun; for others, rather uncomfortable.

Non-Korean Spouses Of Koreans

A number of inter-racial marriages exist between Koreans and westerners, the majority between Korean women and western men, though the reverse also happens. The couples and their families are in the unique position of having one foot in the door of Korean society, and the other foot out.

The logistics of living in Korea can be managed more successfully when one person in the family is fluent in the language and knowledgeable about the culture. There will also probably be the support of friends and family of the Korean spouse, who can ease the transition into Korea. There is usually, in addition, a vested interest in living in Korea and learning about Korean culture.

It sometimes happens, though, that these couples have trouble understanding and accepting each other's culture shock. Koreans who have lived abroad for any length of time will experience a different kind of adjustment problem that an insensitive non-Korean spouse may brush off as not important. The Korean spouse may misinterpret some of the non-Korean's unhappiness in the country as criticism of Korea, and essentially of that partner's roots. Children in such families may be confused about their identities. Families in this situation need to pay special attention to the experiences of other family members.

Interracial Marriage

One difficulty is the stigma attached to inter-racial marriages. Though this prejudice is diminishing with time, many Koreans still look down on people who marry out of their own culture. This is particularly true when the woman is Korean and the man western. Strangers on the street may make derogatory comments about such couples, which are quite unpleasant to hear

In these inter-racial marriages, there is also potential for family-in-law difficulties. Korean families are very close, and generally want to be intimately involved in one another's lives. The non-Korean spouse needs to be aware of traditional Korean family behaviour. At the same time, the Korean spouse needs to remember that such close involvement is not the norm for people coming from western cultures.

Men and Women in the US Military

Koreans hold mixed views about the United States and about the current role the U.S. military plays in their country. Older Koreans are likely to be appreciative of the assistance the U.S. gave during the Korean War. Younger Koreans, however, are likely to resent the influence that the United States has played in their country's history, particularly the Kwangju Incident in 1980, and more recently the demands made by the International Monetary Fund (1997-1998). The image of the U.S. military is further damaged by regular reports of U.S. soldiers committing acts against Korean citizens. Most Koreans do not support the decision of the U.S. to invade Iraq or the deployment of Korean soldiers to assist in that effort, and few believe that the U.S. is responding to North Korea's nuclear ambitions effectively. Nevertheless, most women and men in the U.S. armed forces have mostly positive experiences with Koreans, suggesting that

Koreans are able to separate individuals from the policies of their governments.

Young Children

Many children adjust to life abroad faster than their parents, but expatriate children in Korea have their own special problems. These vary a lot depending on the age and character of the child.

Young children will be touched, patted and pinched, sometimes in places westerners consider private. Black and blonde children especially will draw attention wherever they go. Pre-school children may at first feel left out, not knowing the language, but before long they will speak Korean quite well. Young children often react to changes by regressing to an earlier stage. They may be especially clingy. Bringing familiar toys and books is a way to ease them into the new environment.

Pre-Teens

Leaving friends will be difficult. Pre-teens are old enough to know they will not be able to do the things they were able to do in their own country. They are, however, old enough to understand different cultures and benefit from becoming educated about the new culture. Before moving to Korea, encourage them to do a little research so that they can be looking for things they have read about. Pre-teens benefit from learning the language. At first your family may become especially close, exploring the new city together and sharing this unique yet stressful experience. Since most children in foreign schools are accustomed to moving, it is likely that your child will quickly become integrated into an international group of children. This opportunity will enrich your child's understanding of the world.

Teens

For teens that have not lived abroad, life in Korea will be an abrupt change from what they were expecting. The familiar teen activities that they have been looking forward to may not be available in Korea. They may need to do some mourning over lost opportunities and being separated from dear friends. Teens are in the middle of forming their identity and learning to be independent. Both of these will be affected by living in a different environment, standing out in a crowd. Teens are likely to be angry, perhaps at their parents, when things are tough for them. Fortunately, most teens do adjust and come to appreciate an experience in a new country. They learn how to navigate a whole new culture which gives them confidence for managing a variety of new experiences in the future. Schools for expatriate teens, while providing different experiences than the may have in their own country, are geared specifically for them and meet the needs of most teens.

Third Culture Children

Children whose parents have committed to an international career, spend most or all of their lives away from their home country. They develop skills for living in two or more cultures and become comfortable interacting in a cross-cultural settings. They understand different value systems and recognise that there are many ways to do the same thing. They also quickly bond to other people who have, like them, spent their formative years away from their home country; they understand one another. They are likely to have lifelong friends living all over the world and are likely to choose a life that allows them to travel internationally. For them, staying in one culture seems abnormal.

While third culture kids in some ways know who they are better than their counterparts back home, they become different from those back home. Popular culture and language idioms may be unknown to them. They also will not share the sense of their own country with their parents. Mother and father will have memories of national holidays, particular extended family traditions and school customs that third culture kids do not have. Parents will be quite comfortable returning to their country and, after some time, adjust quite easily to living in that familiar landscape. Third culture kids will not feel that 'home' is really home. For them it is a place to visit, but not a place where they feel that they belong. Growing up abroad certainly has its advantages but parents need to recognise that their children have had a rich experience that sets them apart from their counterparts at home and, in another sense, from the very parents they shared their formative years with.

It is frustrating to always be identified as someone you are not. The reason for this confusion is that the majority of expatriates in Korea are from the United States. And most of the foreign movies shown in Korea are from the United States. In fact, the Korean term for 'American' has all but replaced the term for 'foreigner'.

Westerners Who are Not from the US

Many Koreans assume that anyone who is not Asian is from the United States. British, French and Australians get tired of hearing '*Meegook Sahram*' (United States person) from children on the street.

People Of African Ancestry

People of African descent have a wide range of experiences in Korea. Most Koreans have little knowledge of people of African descent and the little that they do know is likely to be negative. If you have grown up in a culture that discriminates against you, you are familiar with standing out and may find that being different in yet another culture is something you are quite adept at doing. The majority of people of African descent in Korea are people in the U.S. Military so Koreans will likely hold that assumption about you.

People of Korean Ancestry Who Did Not Grow Up in Korea

People of Korean ancestry who were born or lived much of their lives outside Korea have special problems which impact culture shock. Many come to Korea to learn about their roots. Adopted children want to learn the language, or see the country of their birth. Second and third generation Koreans from other countries have perhaps grown up eating some Korean foods, and learning some Korean customs, and they may have come here to meet their relatives. Such Koreans have a special interest in Korea, and a particular eagerness to understand and accept Korean culture.

Koreans respond differently to foreigners with Korean heritage. When a western-looking expatriate speaks elementary Korean in a taxi, for example, the driver is especially pleased that he has made an effort to learn the language. But when a person of Korean ancestry speaks a little hesitant Korean, the driver may blame his parents for not teaching their child Korean, even when the person's adoptive parents are non-Korean.

The same is true of dress style and behaviour. Whereas other westerners can be excused for dressing and behaving in a manner different from Koreans, no such excuses would be offered on behalf of people of Korean blood.

The restrictions of Korean society apply to people of Korean descent, but so do some of the benefits. Non-Koreans, however long they live in the country, will never be totally accepted in Korean society. People of Korean ancestry, on the other hand, even though they think and act like their western-looking counterparts, can sometimes be accepted in Korea. They are included in the group '*uri nara sahram*' or 'our country's people'. It may be hard for such expatriates to establish close relationships, but once they do, there can be a closer bond. This special closeness applies only to people who share the Korean cultural and biological heritage.

Parents Of Children Adopted From Korea

Koreans generally feel sad for parents who have adopted children from Korea, assuming that the reason for adopting was that they could not have given birth to biological children. Koreans also assume adoptive parents to be very loving and generous to give a home to children who are not genetically related. Koreans also feel a sense of shame that they have not provided care for all children of Korean ancestry. Koreans historically have not adopted children who did not have blood ties but this is slowly changing and today support groups exist in Korea for adoptive parents and for adopted Korean children being raised in their own country.

Japanese

As a result of the early Japanese invasions of the southern coast, and their more recent annexation of Korea, Koreans do not hold Japan or the Japanese in highest esteem. The stereotype of Japanese people is that they are wealthy and clean but do not recognise the past crimes they have committed against other Asians. Japanese expatriates living in Korea may have hurdles to overcome.

Other Asians

Some Asians have the distinct advantage of being able to blend in with Koreans. Koreans, even in rural areas do not stare at Asians, nor will they go up to them to practise conversation. The advantage can turn into a disadvantage as soon as an Asian starts to speak. Koreans expect Asians to speak Korean. They may sometimes even think such people are only pretending not to understand Korean for their own advantage. As Korean labour costs have gone up, more foreign workers have come to Korea to work from countries with lower labour costs such as Pakistan, China and the Philippines. Since such workers are likely to be less educated and have less money than Koreans or Japanese, people from these countries are viewed less favourably and are likely to experience less respectful treatment than expatriates of European ancestry.

> Negative reactions in Korea are especially hurtful as these same people are identified as Korean in their home country, and may have believed that in South Korea they could finally belong. Once in Korea, they realise that culturally they are not Korean at all. It is also more difficult for people of Korean ancestry to deal with negative aspects of living in Korea. As they are often identified as Korean, they want it to be a country they can be proud of. They have a stake in liking this country.

Foreigners Who Have Extensive Knowledge of Korea

Some expatriates living in Korea are quite familiar with the Korean language and/or culture. Koreans assume if you look foreign that you know nothing about Korea. Such expatriates tire of hearing compliments about how well they use chopsticks or being warned that *kimchee* is spicy.

When one has knowledge of Korea and can manage the culture quite well one would prefer to use those skills and fit in instead of being treated as a child who knows little. Patience is required.

REVERSE CULTURE SHOCK

Strange as it may seem, returning to one's own culture is likely to be difficult. For many, reverse culture shock is more problematic than the culture shock one experienced moving to another culture. One becomes accustomed to the Korean way of doing things, and may even forget how people in one's own country dress, for example, on a particular type of occasion. One also may find that life in one's own culture is rather dull compared to the rich cultural experiences one had in Korea among Koreans and expatriates from a variety of countries. One is no longer the interesting foreigner one was while living in Korea.

Reverse Shock

Having lived in Korea for many years, I was accustomed to anyone speaking English to be speaking to me. To my surprise, when I returned to my own country I found myself thinking everyone was talking to me. I was in a dressing room and overhead someone say "What do you think of this dress?" and assumed this stranger was asking for my opinion. It took me quite a while to not instinctively respond to anyone speaking English as if they were talking to me.

Also, people who have not lived abroad are not likely to understand an important aspect of one's new identity and friends and family are likely to tire very quickly of hearing about how things are done in Korea. Keeping in contact with friends from Korea is helpful in easing the transition back home.

EATING AND DRINKING

CHAPTER 6

'When one is deciding on whether to eat or
do something else, eating should take priority.'
—A Korean Proverb

FOOD OCCUPIES A CENTRAL PLACE IN THE LIVES OF KOREANS. Koreans sometimes greet each other in the morning "Have you eaten rice?" dating back to a time when everyone didn't always have breakfast. Among Koreans there seems to be a preoccupation with food that goes beyond mere enjoyment and becomes directly connected to health. Korean national media regularly report on new discoveries about health and food and after such reports, millions of Koreans eat more or less of a particular food or prepare a food in a more healthy way. In Korea, giving a person food demonstrates care for another's wellbeing.

Drinking alcoholic beverages is also central to most men's and some women's lives—seeming to contradict the priority Koreans give health. Expatriates in Korea are universally struck by the amount of alcohol that people drink and the important role it plays in work and interpersonal relationships.

This chapter will introduce you to Korean food, including dishes popular among Koreans and expatriates alike. The Korean table will be described, preparing you for how to eat Korean food at a Korean restaurant or in a Korean home. The next section will address issues associated with eating out at a restaurant, including the availability of international cuisines in Korea. Drinking will then be examined, including the complex drinking customs that Koreans adhere to. The chapter will end with guidelines for eating at a Korean home and for inviting Koreans to your home.

FOOD

Korean food is healthy, colourful and flavourful, and most meals include an abundance of seasoned vegetables and lesser amounts of fish, meat and/or soy protien. Koreans eat palatable and often spicy side dishes, served attractively with either their staple, rice, or in some instances, noodles. Koreans depend heavily upon the spices they use when cooking everything from cucumber to fish and beef. These include one or more of the following: red pepper, garlic, green onion, soy sauce and sesame oil. Compared to Japanese food, Korean food has less salt and compared to Chinese food, Korean food uses little oil. Korean food may appear strange to expatriates at first, but it is rare to find someone who does not eventually succumb and enjoy it immensely. Even expatriates who avoid spicy food are sure to find dishes they enjoy. Perhaps that is why Korean restaurants are starting to appear all over the world—the variety of colours, textures, tastes and smells are sure to have something that pleases every palate.

As a guest in Korea, you are likely to be encouraged to eat more than you want. Koreans have no wish for expatriates to get fat (though there is real danger of this, given the delicious food on offer); they are just showing their concern that you stay healthy. Fortunately, it is also polite not to eat everything that is offered.

Making Time for Meals

I recently took a four hour train trip that Koreans in both Seoul and Busan helped me plan. When deciding which train to take, the Seoul and Busan friends both paid great attention to making sure I would have time to eat—something that I alone would not have considered when selecting a train. As soon as I arrived, I was immediately asked if I had eaten. Food is such a high priority for Koreans.

TYPICAL KOREAN FOOD

Koreans make no distinction between the type of food they eat for breakfast, lunch and dinner, and short-grained rice is central to most meals, usually eaten with various side dishes. During times of hardship, the poor, not being able to afford white rice, had to settle for cooked barley, which was much cheaper. In the past five years, for health reasons, many Koreans have started eating mixed grains and beans instead of white rice. This assortment of grains, which can be bought together or separately, include such ingredients as brown rice, wild rice, barley, hulled millet, green peas, kidney beans and small read beans. Since these grains and beans are more expensive than white rice, those with a strict food budget are limited to just white rice.

To know Korean food is to know *kimchee*, a spicy, pickled vegetable dish, which is served with virtually every meal. *Kimchee* can be made of almost any vegetable, but usually it is made of Chinese or *napa* cabbage which is rinsed with salt water and left to ferment overnight. Spices and herbs, including garlic, red pepper, green onion and ginger, are then added. Before refrigerators were available, it was made in autumn after the harvest and put in underground pots so that vegetables would be available throughout the winter. Traditionally, *kimchee* in the autumn, called *Kimchang*, was an indispensable and laborious task. Anyone who has tasted *kimchee* will know it has an indescribable, distinctive taste as well as a strong smell. This has caused some problems for Korean students studying abroad as the smell of *kimchee* can permeate a dormitory refrigerator.

Families have their own particular *kimchee* preferences, with more or less of particular seasoning differentiating them. In addition, the dish sours as it ages so individuals have preferences for *kimchee* at different points in the aging process.

Besides rice and *kimchee*, every meal includes soup, the only liquid served. The soup may contain a number of items, such as fish, bean paste, beef and *mung* beansprouts.

All the other foods at the meal are called *pan chan* or side dishes. Usually this includes a variety of vegetables, lightly cooked with the Korean spices, and may or may not include fish, pork or beef. Soup and rice should always be steaming hot but the other dishes may be warm, at room temperature or even cold. Though beef used to be relatively expensive, and used primarily for special occasions, it is now reasonably priced but also recognised as less healthy than fish.

For the Love of Kimchee
An American was captured by the North Koreans during the Korean War. He spent five years in a North Korean prison. When he was released, so the story goes, he had become so accustomed to *kimchee* that one of the first things he told his wife was "You have got to learn how to make kimchee." Koreans are very glad to hear that foreigners like their national food.

At times, noodles are also eaten in place of rice. There is a wide variety of rice and noodles, with some made at home and ready-to-cook noodles available in the market. *Ramen* noodles, seasoned to the Korean tastes, are a cheap and easy meal, though not known for their nutritional value.

Korean Foods to Try

- **Bee Bim Bap** A huge bowl is filled with rice, and small piles of various colourful vegetables are layered on top. A barely cooked egg sits to one side. Koreans add a generous amount of hot pepper paste to their individual bowls and mix it all together.
- **Bulgogi** Thin strips of beef that have been marinated in soy sauce, garlic, green onions and sugar, are barbecued, often right at your table. This food is served on special occasions. Since Koreans have correctly heard that foreigners like this food and because they wish to offer guests the best, expatriates tend to be served *bulgogi* often.
- **Chop Chae** A mixture of clear noodles and a variety of cut-up vegetables and meat, this is a dish expatriates invariably fall in love with.
- **Kalbi** Barbecued beef ribs, prepared similarly to *bulgogi*.
- **Kalbi Chim** This is a kind of beef rib casserole. The beef is seasoned as it is in *kalbi*, then simmered with carrots, mushrooms, chestnuts and potatoes.

- **Kim** Most expatriates learn to love this seaweed. It is sometimes wrapped around vegetables and seasoned rice to make *kim bap*, a common food to take on picnics.
- **Mandoo** These small dumplings filled with tasty vegetables and meat originated in China. They are served in a hot soup (*man doo gook*), fried (*goon man doo*) or steamed (*jjin man doo*). There are special shops that serve only *man doo* and *kimchee*.
- **Naeng Myun** This summer dish, whose name means 'cold noodles', consists of cold buckwheat noodles in cold beef broth. Strips of beef, half a hard-boiled egg and/or vegetables are included. Since many small eateries are not careful about sanitation, many Koreans will eat this only at a reputable place.
- **Kimbap** This is a favourite picnic food but can be eaten at other times as well. It is similar to Japanese *sushi* but does not contain raw fish. Strips of vegetables, such as carrots and spinach, and perhaps meat and egg, are surrounded by seasoned rice and wrapped in seaweed paper.

Tips for Eating a Korean Meal
- Other than rice and soup, all food is shared.
- A spoon is used for rice and soup; chopsticks for all else
- Everyone can eat what appeals to them; avoid what doesn't
- Sometimes the host will put especially tasty morsels of food in your bowl
- It's okay to finish all the soup and rice; it's not okay to finish all other food on table
- While eating, rest your chopsticks/spoon on a bowl
- When finished, set your chopsticks/spoon on the table

TABLE MANNERS
Traditionally, the men of the house were served first. They ate on low, lacquered tables that were set in the kitchen and carried into another room for the meal. (Koreans used the same room for eating, visiting and sleeping.) Korean women traditionally sat by the men, watching them as they ate, ready to get them anything else they needed.

Only when the men were finished would the women and children eat.

Typical Table Setting

- Everyone has an individual rice bowl.
- Two chopsticks (often metal) are placed to the right of the rice bowl.
- One large, shallow spoon is placed to the right of the chopsticks.
- Individual *gook* (soup) bowls are put to the right of the rice bowl.
- Multiple small dishes are served with a wide variety of bite-sized, seasoned vegetables, fish and meat.

These days, men, women and children usually eat together. Most families today use western style table and chairs but the traditional low table may be used for special meals such as holidays or when guests come. Hot rice is served in individual bowls, placed to the left of the diner, and soup is served in another bowl, always to the right of the rice. The various side dishes are set on small plates. If there are very

Many Koreans today enjoy eating special meals in the traditional way, sitting on cushions at low tables.

many people, two or more plates of the same food are set out to make passing unnecessary. Stainless steel or silver chopsticks are used, with a large soup spoon.

The most honoured person (usually the oldest) takes the first bite. During meals, it is considered impolite to talk much; the food should be enjoyed without distraction. This silence may seem strange to expatriates. In fact, the meal is not silent. To show your appreciation of the food, slurping of soup and noodles is totally acceptable. Some older Koreans burp at the end of the meal, as a sign of satisfaction.

Seasonal fruit is served at the end of the meal, cut into small pieces. It is eaten with a fork or toothpicks. (Eating any food with fingers is considered impolite.) Sweets and desserts are generally eaten as snacks, not during main meals.

Eating Prohibitions
- Don't eat before the oldest person
- Don't pick up a rice or soup bowl to eat
- Don't stick chopsticks vertically into the rice bowl
- Don't blow your nose
- Don't talk much during the meal: focus on enjoying the food and talk later
- Don't leave the table before oldest person

EATING OUT
Eating out is a common Korean pastime and there are meals and restaurants to suit every taste and budget. Expatriates, too, are sure to find an endless number of enjoyable places if they live in a metropolitan area. Besides Korean food, Seoul, in particular, holds a wide array of international restaurants, including Chinese, Japanese, Italian, French, Mexican, Thai, Vietnamese, Indian and Middle Eastern and a few vegetarian restaurants. Some of these include international chains. If you have a craving for a particular variety of food, Koreans have restaurants catering towards dumplings, noodles, barbeque meat and *sushi*. Fast food restaurants abound and simple sandwiches or *sushi* (which is called *kimbap*) can be bought at convenience shops.

Red peppers, an important ingredient of many Korean foods, drying on a straw mat.

More exclusive Korean and Japanese restaurants generally seat people at low tables and sometimes in private rooms. Guests sit on soft pillows and tend to put their feet to the side, though you can also put them straight in front of you if you wish. In such rooms, shoes are prohibited and taken off before stepping into (and often up to) the room. Koreans feel comfortable and intimate in such rooms and it is likely that once you have experienced this style of eating you will also like it.

Smoking

Though Korea has begun to have non-smoking sections in some of their restaurants, it is quite common for other diners to light up after a meal—even, sometimes, in non-smoking sections. If you are a smoker, you will find this to your advantage.

Dog Meat Restaurants

Many have heard that Koreans eat dog meat and this is true. However, dog is not a common food and most Koreans have never eaten dog. People do not cook dog at home: it is only served at restaurants which specialise in this kind of meat. You will not be inadvertently served dog when eating out or in someone's home and people certainly do not catch dogs on the street and cook them. Dog meat is primarily eaten by men who want to increase their energy and/or increase their sexual stamina.

Who Pays?

In Korea the rule is quite simple: the person who invites pays. Even among close friends, it is considered impolite to 'go Dutch'. Anyone close enough to eat a meal with someone would certainly be willing and eager to pay for the meal and the person with the highest status tends to do the inviting and the paying. Among Korean men and women of equal status, there seems to be a kind of unspoken calculation so that all people end up treating each other to an equal amount. It is also quite common for people of a lesser status and means to treat their superiors when the cost is lower. For example, after an expensive meal has been paid for by the higher status person, the lesser status person may then pay for coffee at a different restaurant.

Tipping

Tips are not expected in Korea. Guests are treated kindly because they are guests, and not with the expectation of gaining a tip. Hotels do add a 10 per cent service charge and a 10 per cent tax on to the bill automatically. The money paid to hostesses who accompany customers is also called a tip, but it is often set in advance. It is not necessary to tip anywhere else.

Going To Multiple Establishments

It is quite common for Koreans to frequent several places in the course of an evening. First, they may meet at a café, whilst waiting for everyone to arrive. Next, they might move to a place to eat the main course of the meal, followed by one, or more commonly several, drinking places. Individuals take turns at paying the whole bill at each establishment.

DRINKING

While the role of alcohol has diminished somewhat in recent years, for many Korean men drinking remains an integral part of having fun. Whether attending a one-hundred-day celebration, camping out, socialising or trying to establish an amicable business relationship, liquor is almost indispensable, at least for men. High quality beers, hard liquor, an increasing number of wines and traditional Korean alcoholic beverages are the most popular.

Alcoholic Beverages Unique to Korea

- Soju: a clear, cheap and strong beverage much like vodka
- Makkoli: a milky-white drink popular amongst students
- Chong-jong: a rice wine
- Popchu: a higher quality rice wine

Purpose

Any reason is a good reason for saying '*Han chan hapshida!*' ('Let's have a drink.') Many Korean men believe that the best way to get to know a person is to drink with him. They believe that adults show the world a kind of mask, appearing to be as others expect them to be. To know a person's true self, they must see him 'under the influence'.

Drinking is often a necessary prelude to most business. It may be difficult to trust a business partner until a few drinks have been shared. Sometimes the only way to resolve a sensitive problem or close a touchy business deal is over a generous amount of wine. People who do not drink as much as their counterparts are sometimes thought to be hiding something, afraid to let down their defences. Many Koreans would prefer not to drink so much, but not to drink, or to stop drinking too soon might ruin the mood for everyone. In terms of etiquette, it is particularly difficult for someone of a lower status to turn down a request to drink from someone of a higher status.

This emphasis on drinking for social and business reasons goes back to the Unified Shilla period, if not before. There are even Confucian ceremonies demonstrating the proper way to become drunk. Fortunately, there is a trend today amongst younger Koreans to move away from such heavy drinking. Abstinence or moderate consumption is more acceptable in the younger crowds than it is for people in the older generation. Still, drinking continues to pervade many aspects of the lives of most Korean males.

Drinking Customs
The expatriate may be baffled the first time he goes drinking with a Korean. Your friend will be happy to show you Korean drinking customs and if you get it wrong, Koreans will understand as long as it is clear you are trying hard to learn. Eventually it will become second nature to you.

Drinking Rules
- The person of lower status, or the host of the event, will offer an empty glass to the most honoured person.
- If the status or age difference is very great, he will offer the glass with two hands, or support the right hand with the left.
- The person receiving the glass, depending on his status, will also receive it with two hands or with the right supported by the left.
- The giver then pours the alcohol into the glass held by the receiver.
- As the drinking continues, everyone is offered a glass, which is then filled.
- After one finishes one's own glass, it is customary to give the same glass to another person. During the course of an evening, people are careful to exchange glasses with everyone else.
- One should not add alcohol to a glass that is partially filled, or fill one's own glass.

Luckily, with all this drinking, food is also consumed. Appetisers, collectively called *anjoo*, may include dried beef, dried fish, nuts or even fruit. Some places offer an *anjoo* menu. At other places, *anjoo* is brought to your table even if it is not ordered, but be careful as it is not free of charge.

Refusing A Drink
Considering the amount of alcohol imbibed, there may be times when one is tempted to refuse. This borders on anti-social behaviour. Koreans have the same problem, as there

is often one person urging everyone else to drink one more glass, but being Koreans, they go ahead and drink, even if it means becoming sick.

An expatriate has the advantage of being able to fall back on his culture, to some extent, to minimise his drinking. A wife at home is a better excuse for an expatriate than for a Korean. Some foreigners and Koreans have poured unwanted alcohol surreptitiously into a local plant. In less refined establishments, alcohol could be spilt, quite discreetly, of course. Holding a full glass and drinking slowly also makes it less likely that another will be poured for you. If all else fails, you can say you are taking traditional Korean *hanyak* (medicine) and so cannot drink. You may also say your religion prohibits or discourages consuming alcohol. This is an acceptable excuse among Korean men but it also make social relationships more difficult.

Drinking Behaviour

While some degree of control should be kept, no matter how much is consumed, one sometimes sees a person who, by western standards, has lost control. Physical fights, loud arguing and men supporting their far-gone drinking buddy are features of popular drinking areas. In apartment blocks, understanding neighbours are expected to tolerate loud laughter, singing and fights. It is unthinkable to call the police to curb the disturbance and most drunken bad behaviour is excused—drinking is considered an acceptable way to deal with pent up frustration or anger.

The Role of Women in Social Drinking

Traditionally, a good Korean woman didn't drink. However, this custom is changing, especially among college women who often enjoy drinking alongside their male classmates. Younger, married women can be found drinking moderately with their friends or husbands, but serious drinking is still mostly left to the men.

Women who are found in some drinking establishments are considered to be a different sort. These young, beautiful females are hired to sit with an equal number of men, pour their drinks and make friendly conversation. The price of their company is not cheap so usually it is paid for by the man's boss but do not confuse them with prostitutes. It goes without saying that wives and girlfriends are not welcome at such places.

GISAENGS

Gisaengs, dressed in traditional Korean clothes and found only in *gisaeng* houses, have a long and important history in Korea. They used to be the only educated women in the country. Not only could they write poetry and practise Chinese calligraphy, but they also sang and danced. Trained in special schools, their job was to entertain aristocrats at parties and functions.

While these women were always from the lowest social class, there are several instances of *gisaengs* who became heroines. One story goes how, after the Japanese invaded the southern coast of Korea in the late 15th century, the famous *gisaeng,* Non-Gae, entertained a Japanese general. She convinced him to take a walk along a cliff by a river. At an opportune moment, she clasped her arms around the general and fell into the river with him where they both died. You can still visit the spot in Jinju.

While the number of *gisaengs* has substantially diminished, elegant *gisaeng* houses still exist in Korea. Gracious women pour drinks, put morsels into their customers' mouths, dance and sing. These houses are extremely expensive, with bills sometimes running into thousands of US dollars for a small group of people. Companies usually entertain potential clients in the splendour of *gisaeng* houses but because of the high cost, it is rare today for expatriates to visit such places.

SINGING

As mentioned already, when Koreans drink, it is rarely just one beer after a hard day's work. Oblivious to the responsibility of work the morning after, drinking often continues until late into the night and, as the evening progresses, the most honoured person will be usually be asked to sing a solo.

To the expatriate, this can be quite an unnerving experience. It does not matter if you cannot sing: just make sure you know the words to one short song. There have been cases when an innocent foreigner has managed to avoid singing, but remember this is done at some social cost. It is far better to sing a few lines of 'Row, row, row your boat' or 'Twinkle, twinkle, little star' and be done with it.

Sometimes, listening to other singers can be worse than singing yourself. The majority of Koreans sing exceptionally well, and their presentation can be interesting, but when all you want to do is go home, and every one of your 15 companions is waiting to perform, you will not find it so entertaining.

The karaoke bar, called a *noraebang* or singing room, is widely enjoyed in Korea by people of all ages. Most *noraebangs* have rooms where groups of 10-20 people can gather in front of a video screen which flashes words to music, including some English songs. For a few moments, the most ordinary person can pretend to be a famous singer. The room is paid for by the hour and you can buy alcoholic beverages or soft drinks and snacks.

BEING INVITED TO A KOREAN HOME

In the past decades, it has become less common for Koreans to entertain people in their home and more commonly, they will invite people to a restaurant. Being invited to someone's home is a great honour and guests always hold a special place in Korean society. Special food is prepared for a visitor and no expense is considered too great. The main concern of host and hostess is that you enjoy yourself, eat well and feel comfortable.

Invitations

Last-minute invitations are the norm. Traditionally, women did not accompany their husbands to social functions but these days they are sometimes included, though the invitation, even if it is written, will probably not mention the fact. If you ask your host, he will say that of course your wife is included, but she may then turn out to be the only female guest. It is

best to ask another person who has also been invited and if no one else's wife has been included you have no choice but to ask the host. Children are rarely included in such invitations. To show respect to a host and hostess, you should dress decently, men in a suit and tie, women in a dress or elegant trousers.

Arriving

People are often invited to someone's home in a group. It is usual for the guests to arrange to gather at one spot, then proceed to their host's address. This is particularly true when no spouses are included. Sometimes meeting together first is done to help those who do not know the way and it does make it more convenient for the host.

Do not worry if you are unable to arrive at the specified time. Arriving 10 to 15 minutes late is alright, but being more than 30 minutes late is insulting. Never arrive early, however, as it may cause some embarrassment.

Koreans greet their guests at the entrances to their homes. As they do not wear shoes indoors, you should remove yours at the door. Expatriate women have learnt to wear slip-on shoes, but the men cannot get around the awkward tying

Slippers

On occasions, as you enter the house, you will observe slippers set out for guests. If the floor is cold, these will provide insulation can also serve as protection from unpleasant falls on slippery wooden Korean floors. However, you may choose not to wear them.

and untying of laces. (Remember to check your socks for holes, however; as walking around all evening in holey socks can be embarrassing.)

Gifts

Visiting empty-handed is impolite. The usual gift is a box or bag of fruit, bought at the local fruit stand. A gift from a bakery or florist's is also appropriate. For a host who enjoys his drinking, alcohol makes an excellent gift, particularly if it is a foreign brand. Gift-wrapped boxes of fruit juice make suitable gifts and if there is a child, a small toy would be well-received. Gifts that can be wrapped should be wrapped and often Koreans put a wrapped gift inside a tasteful shop bag if the gift is from a respectable shop. Koreans do not open gifts in front of the giver.

Inappropriate gifts are money, towels and decorative items for the home. Do not bring a gift in your own container, such as home-made cookies on a plate, as your hostess will then feel obligated to fill the container before returning it to you. Pot luck dinners have not caught on in Korea, so do not bring or offer to bring any part of the meal.

The Meal

Guests invited to a Korean home are invariably served a meal. Sometimes drinks or fruit juice and an appetiser will be offered in the living room, but most meals will be given in the master bedroom, called the *anbang*. Being invited into the master bedroom is an honour.

A low table will be set up in this room but if there are many guests, several low tables will be placed end to end. Seating is on large, soft cushions. The whole meal will be served at the same time, with rice and soup next to individual plates and all side dishes spread out in the centre.

Before the meal, the host or hostess often says 'We do not have much to eat, but please eat a lot.' It reflects the Korean attitude that even the biggest feast is not good enough for

A group of women enjoy a dinner at traditional low tables. Koreans experience them as more friendly and comfortable than western style tables.

their guests. Alcohol is likely to be served both before, with and after the meal.

Before the meal, conversation is amicable, but when the main course is taken, talking is unusual, as people are focusing completely on the delicious food. The host or hostess will encourage you to eat and will be pleased to see you enjoy yourself. This is again a Korean expression of concern. You may be obliged to eat more than you wish.

After The Meal

As soon as the main meal is over, coffee is served with cut fruit. By this time, the male guests should be loosening up with the effects of alcohol, and talk will be quite pleasant.

If you are the most honoured guest, you will soon be asked to sing. This is a sincere request, so prepare a song ahead of time. Pleading a poor voice is not an acceptable excuse. Often, as one sings, the others will clap or join in.

Leaving

Singing and drinking can continue for several hours. The longer guests stay, the more assured is the host that they are enjoying themselves. When the guests are ready to leave, the host and hostess will accompany them to the door.

After guests have put on their shoes, they face the host and hostess, bow and say goodbye. Sometimes the host will accompany them to the front gate, in which case the bowing takes place there.

ENTERTAINING KOREANS AT YOUR HOME

Koreans are very pleased to be invited to someone's home. They sincerely appreciate any effort you make to treat them kindly, to feed them or make them comfortable. Any blunders will be overlooked. Here are a few tips from experienced expatriates to help your entertaining go smoothly.

Invitations

While Koreans who have lived in other countries are accustomed to formal, written invitations, in Korea people are usually invited informally, with little advance notice, sometimes only a few hours before the event. Most expatriate wives would prefer to give a little notice, but invitations given more than a week in advance may be forgotten.

It is only recently that Korean women began accompanying their husbands to some social functions and some Korean men and women are still uncomfortable about doing this, so even when you invite women, they may not come. You will probably not be notified of this in advance.

Though you may ask your guests to come at a particular time, they may be a little late. In unusual cases, they may arrive up to an hour late. It is important to have a flexible menu, bearing in mind the possible delay in serving time.

Greetings

It is a Korean custom to greet guests as they arrive. Even if you are in the middle of something important, drop everything and go to the entrance to welcome your guests. The hostess will graciously accept any gift, then return to her work while the host makes the guests comfortable.

Drinks and Appetisers

Guests should be served some food and drink from a tray as soon as they arrive. It is better to use an unopened bottle of liquor as this gives the impression that you bought the alcohol just for them. The host should pour drinks for his guests in their presence and the hostess should never do the pouring; in the Korean context this is done only by bar hostesses and would make Koreans feel uncomfortable.

While you can ask guests for their choice of drink, they may not answer you, or they may say they do not want anything. Refusing is considered polite. You should give them something anyhow. Female guests may be given alcohol, but do not expect them to drink much.

It is appropriate to serve a wide variety of appetisers. Korean appetisers or *anjoo* are readily available and please everyone. They include dried fish, dried meat, nuts, raisins and roasted seaweed. Biscuits and crisps are not considered elegant. Some non-Korean appetisers that are well received are Japanese *sushi*, devilled eggs and oysters. Cheese is popular among Korean children, but is not eaten by many adults.

The Dinner Menu

Be prepared to serve a banquet: your Korean guests deserve special food. Not only should the quality be excellent, but there should be an ample amount for everyone. Koreans may feel insulted or unwelcome if they are served what they consider to be only a few items.

With the exception of those who have travelled abroad, many Koreans are apprehensive about eating non-Korean food. They are delighted, however, if you hire someone to prepare the meal, Korean- style. Whoever you hire to prepare the food will probably know what to prepare. Serving beef is important; pork or chicken alone would be insulting. Koreans usually serve *bulgogi* or *kalbi*. *Chop chae* is always popular, and a fish or chicken dish would go down well. There must also be numerous other side dishes, and never forget the rice, soup and *kimchee*!

If you think your guests would prefer to eat western food, an imported ham might be a good main course. Steaks or any other beef dishes would also be enjoyed. Most western vegetables, on the other hand, are tasteless to Koreans, but a particularly spicy vegetable dish should please them. Most Koreans also enjoy breads.

Many expatriate hosts and hostesses have discovered that a combination of Korean and non-Korean food works best. That way, timid eaters can stick to the Korean food, which the hired help can prepare. A few speciality dishes from your own country would then add an exotic flavour to the meal. Even if the guests do not know what to make of your spinach soufflé, they will appreciate the trouble you have taken for them.

Serving the Meal

While many first-rate hotels in Korea serve expensive and elegant buffets, people generally do not serve buffet-style in their homes. Being served at a table is more gracious and since expatriates' homes are usually not set up in the Korean style, service at a western table is also more convenient.

The Natural Order

There is no need to assign places. People will naturally sit down where they feel comfortable. Guests will probably sit near people of the same sex.

If Korean food is being served, chopsticks should be provided. Even expatriates feel that it is strange to eat *kimchee* with a fork! Any kind of table setting will work, but a nice one would be appreciated.

Alcohol may be served throughout the meal, and care should be taken to refill empty glasses. Other beverages are usually not drunk until after. Koreans themselves serve water at the end of the meal so it may be easiest to place a glass of water beside each plate at the beginning of the meal.

Dessert

Koreans always appreciate fruit after their meal, no matter how full they are. Fruit such as apples, peaches and pears should be peeled, cut to bite-size pieces and attractively arranged on serving plates with tiny forks. Coffee or tea would be appropriate at the same time.

If you enjoy making desserts, you can serve home-baked items in small pieces with the fruit. Koreans generally would not serve sweets after a meal, but they would almost certainly be very appreciative of any you prepare.

After the Meal

If you have urged your guests to eat more than they intended, you have succeeded in being a good host. After the meal your guests will most likely continue to eat and talk. Make sure there is always some kind of food available for them to eat as taking all the food away immediately conveys an impolite message: that it is time for them to depart.

At a Korean party, people would start to sing, but they may feel inhibited in an expatriate's home. If you enjoy this custom, you could encourage the most honoured guest to begin the 'recital'.

Bidding Guests Farewell

Korean guests will leave your house at the same time. As the host and hostess, you should accompany them to the door. It would be even more thoughtful to escort them to your gate or to the area outside your home or flat. According to Korean custom, a host or hostess who bids their guests goodbye from inside the house is insulting them. Having said goodbye properly, you can then relax inside your suddenly quiet home, knowing that if any mistakes were inadvertently made, they will be forgiven.

ENJOYING YOUR EXPERIENCE IN KOREA

CHAPTER 7

'Over the mountains, more mountains.'
—A Korean Proverb

EXPATRIATES LIVING IN KOREA have an abundance of activities to do. As Korea is a relatively small country, one can get to cultural and travel destinations easily. Other Asian countries can be easily accessed from Seoul or Busan and many expatriates take advantage of visiting those countries while in the vicinity. Since Korea has four distinct seasons, and much travel that Koreans do is related to beauty specific to the season, this chapter will begin with a description of the four seasons. Holidays and festivals in Korea can be wonderful fun for expatriates, and these will also be described. The next section of this chapter will suggest some travel destinations, both in Korea and outside and the last section will discuss unique activities that expatriates have an opportunity to participate in while living in Korea, including public baths.

Korea's beautiful countryside makes the four clear seasons particularly striking with each season lasting about three months. The scenery appears to be changing continually, and if winter seems too cold or summer too long, one can take heart in the fact that the next season is just round the corner.

SPRING

This especially welcome season comes earlier in the south, gradually spreading to the north. The first sign is the bright yellow forsythia flowers which line streets, surround houses and decorate motorways. Then, one by one, other spring flowers make their appearance, resulting in four to six weeks of blooms. The weather is cool at first, and sometimes wet, but gradually becomes warmer.

Small strawberries in the markets are another sign of spring. As the season progresses, they give way to large, lush ones and later to raspberries. With the advent of greenhouses, these fruits now make their appearance a month or two early and by the time the yellow melon appears, one can tell summer is on the way.

Spring is a beautiful time to travel in Korea; the Chinhae Cherry Blossom is an unforgettable sight, as is a visit to any temple, including the temples in urban areas.

SUMMER

The clear spring days are often followed by a two-week spell of rainy weather, beginning at about the end of June. Sometimes the heavy summer rains result in floods.

After the rainy season, the really hot and humid weather begins. This is when straw mats for ventilated seating and the beautiful Korean fans come in handy. Highs in Seoul often reach 26°C (80°F). Cold watermelon and sweet juicy peaches are some consolation in the intense, overbearing heat, which, however, only lasts a few weeks, and sometimes not even that long. Thankfully, most homes, businesses and shops are air conditioned. By the beginning of September, the evenings turn refreshingly cool.

AUTUMN

The height of autumn, much acclaimed by visitors to Korea, lasts a good month. As in spring, there is a progression of colour, making even the humblest home a castle. This season is also an especially good time to explore Korea. The temples, always located on a picturesque mountain, couldn't be more beautiful. Nae Jang San in North Cholla Province is an especially

While I agree that Korea's seasons are distinct and beautiful, I grew tired of being told again and again that "Korea has four seasons". Apparently Koreans are unaware that many other places in the world also have four seasons and are taught from a young age that one of the wonderful things about their country are her four seasons popular place, as is the Sorak Mountain which overlooks the north-eastern coast.

Autumn is marked by crisp, sweet apples in the market, along with the unique Korean pear (in many places it is known as the Asian pear), huge purple grapes and the fragrance of roasting chestnuts on the street.

Traditionally, one of the most important autumn events is Kimjang. This is the time for making the *kimchee* that is to last all winter. Markets are full of mounds of Chinese or *napa* cabbages, radishes, green onions, red peppers and garlic, the main ingredients for *kimchee*. These foods are pickled and stored in the ground in large clay pots. In the warmer southern provinces, more salt is used to preserve the *kimchee*, accounting for the distinct flavour variations in different parts of the country. These days, supermarkets are well stocked with fresh vegetables all year round, so many people do not make as much as they used to. For many Koreans, however, Kimjang *kimchee* is the most delicious variety of the year.

WINTER

Winter is milder in the far southern regions than further north, the snow not even reaching Busan, whilst other regions receive varying amounts of snow. Watching Koreans dispose of snow can baffle the recent arrival as they sweep the it from the curb into the street. Then, as the cars run over it, the snow melts and disappears. In most western countries, the snow would be swept off the streets.

The heating system in Korean homes is unique. A series of pipes lie beneath the floor and hot water (in the older homes, hot air) runs through the pipes, making the floor pleasantly warm. In Korean, this is called an *ondol* floor. As the warmth rises naturally, the Korean tradition of sleeping, eating and sitting on the floor makes this a peculiarly sensible heating system. Most flats and homes where expatriates live are also heated this way and most expatriates appreciate this system. In fact, some custom made homes in the west are also adapting this style of heating.

Kimchee pots store kimchee through the winter. When temperatures drop to freezing, the pots are buried.

In winter, mandarin oranges from Cheju Island are abundant. In late November, a unique citrus fruit, *yooja*, can be bought, layered with honey or sugar and set aside. Then, in the cold winter, it is an especially welcome tea called *yooja cha*.

HOLIDAYS AND FESTIVALS

Koreans know how to celebrate. No expense or energy is considered too great when guests are visiting to celebrate a happy occasion. The tendency is to spend too much, in proportion to income, so as not to offend guests or appear less successful than one would wish. Following the Confucian system, holidays are traditionally celebrated in the oldest family member's home so people do their best to spend important holidays with their elderly parents or grandparents.

New Year's Day, 2-day National Holiday
1–2 January

While Koreans celebrate New Year by the lunar calendar, offices are closed and people celebrate the beginning of the solar New Year.

Seollal (Lunar New Year) 2-day National Holiday
First Day of the First Lunar Month,
Usually in February

This is the most important holiday of the year. All forms of transportation are jammed as people make every effort to travel to their hometowns to honour their parents and enjoy this most festive occasion. An essential feature is bowing deeply to one's ancestors and elders. Food is set before photographs of the family ancestors, and the family members bow deeply, first to them, next to the grandparents, and then to the parents. Younger sons and their wives bow to older brothers and their wives and the children in one nuclear family bow together. This special bowing, called *sae bae*, is often done in traditional clothes, especially by women. Recently, it has become more common to see men in *hanboks* on family holidays.

When children bow deeply to their elders, they are usually given money, called *sae bae tone* (*tone* means money). College-age cousins use this to go to the discos later in the day.

After the *sae bae*, breakfast is served. The food includes *ddok guk* (dumpling soup), rice cakes, fruit, a rice punch called *shikae* and a punch made of dried persimmon and honey called *soo jung gwa*. Two kinds of rice wine are also traditional for this day: *makoli* and *dong dong ju*.

Perhaps more than other holidays, when men often segregate themselves from women and children, this is a day for family activities. One of the most popular games played by Koreans of all ages is *yoot*. Four wooden sticks, one side flat and one side rounded, are thrown up into the air. Players take turns throwing them up and are awarded points, depending on how the wooden sticks land.

Another popular activity in the country, especially for the boys, is kite flying and the brightly coloured kites are strikingly beautiful against the clean white snow. For girls there is the traditional Korean see-saw. (*These and other traditional Korean folk games are described in detail on page 181.*)

On solar New Year's Day, or in the days that follow, if there is time Koreans visit the homes of those they respect. Students will visit teachers, workers, their boss or anyone older who has been (or whom they hope will be) of particular help. These people are honoured by a deep bow. Visits are expected, so each family keeps plenty of refreshments on hand.

Be Prepared

Take a walk in the streets if you are in Korea during the solar and lunar New Years. You will see hundreds of traditional *hanboks* and the excitement in the air is infectious. Be warned, however, that all shops will be boarded up. Stock up on groceries and other essential items.

When invited to a Korean's home, you too can dress in a *hanbok* if you feel comfortable doing so. You may enjoy the family emphasis, which is unlike many western New Year customs, where meeting friends and drinking are the focus.

If you wish to usher in the New Year with a few drinks, several first-class hotels offer enjoyable parties.

Independence Day, National Holiday
1 March
This holiday observes the 1 March 1919 Independence Movement against Japanese colonial rule. There is an annual reading of the Korean Proclamation of Independence.

Arbour Day, National Holiday
5 April
There is an old belief in Korea that anything planted on this day will flourish. After the Korean War, it became especially important as hundreds of mountains had been completely

burned in the hunt for communists. On Arbour Day, you will see groups of government officers, company workers and schoolchildren planting trees. Koreans will often plant trees and flowers in their gardens, and flat dwellers buy flower boxes to bring some nature into the towering cement structures they call home.

Hanshik Day
5 or 6 April

Hanshik literally means 'cold food'. According to legend, long ago in China there lived a man, Kai Ja Chu, who was very loyal to his king. Jealous of his devotion, the other subjects forced him from the king's presence. If Kai Ja Chu could not be with the king, he wanted to live in solitude, so he hid in the mountains. The king searched for him, without success. Upon hearing Kai Ja Chu was hiding in a mountain cave, the king set fire to the mountain to drive him out. Kai Ja Chu died in the fire. In admiration of his loyalty, the remorseful king and people decided to honour him by eating only cold food on the anniversary of the fire, a Chinese custom that eventually came down to Korea.

Today in Korea, this day is often set aside to tend ancestors' graves. The women pack a picnic lunch (not always cold) and the family heads for the burial site, usually on a scenic mountain slope and reached on foot.

At the grave, the ancestral ceremonies are performed and the graves are weeded and reshaped after the winter. While the ceremony is serious, the family thoroughly enjoys the picnic and the beginnings of spring weather. If a family is unable to go to the grave on Hanshik Day, members will designate another day to go.

Children's Day, National Holiday
5 May

It is only to be expected that a country where children are loved so well would surely set aside a special day for them. On this day, children do anything they please: go to amusement parks, visit the zoo, have a picnic or participate in one of the many special programmes organised just for them.

Korean children also receive gifts from their parents on this day. If you have children, they would doubtless be happy if you followed this custom but as on other holidays, be warned that traffic both in and out of the cities will be heavy and places catering for children extremely crowded.

Parents' Day
8 May
This day was traditionally set aside to honour mothers, indicating perhaps the strong affection Koreans have for their own mothers. Somewhere along the way, it became Parents' Day so as not to neglect the fathers. Children often buy a corsage for their mother and some small gift for their father.

Teachers' Day
15 May
Teachers who have a special place in this Confucian-oriented society are honoured on this day. Students give them small gifts or a corsage, and university students sometimes treat their professors to lunch.

Buddha's Birthday, National Holiday
Eighth Day of the Fourth Lunar Month
On this day, Buddhists visit temples to pray. Families buy a colourful lantern, attach a ribbon with the family's names and hang it at the Buddhist temple. In the evening, a lantern parade is held.

Memorial Day, National Holiday
6 June
A day in remembrance of Koreans who died in service to their nation. Memorial services are held at the National Cemetery in Seoul.

Constitution Day, National Holiday
17 July
This day commemorates the adoption of the Constitution for the Republic of Korea in 1948.

Liberation Day, National Holiday
15 August
Besides commemorating the beginning of the Republic of Korea in 1948, this day celebrates the freedom from the Japanese on this same day in 1945.

Chusok, National Holiday
August (Lunar) Three days
Harvest Moon Festival and Korean Thanksgiving are two other names for this holiday, the second most important one in Korea. Families visit ancestors' graves, set out food and bow. Among special foods from the autumn harvest are rice cakes called song pyon, shaped like a half moon.

A dance performed at this time, especially popular in South Cholla Province, is the *kanggang suwolae*. It originated when the Japanese were invading the southern coast during the 16th century and Korean women joined hands in a circle and danced around, to give the impression to distant Japanese soldiers that there were many Korean soldiers.

The Chusok moon is supposed to be the most beautiful of the year, so many people stroll outdoors to enjoy the bright full moon.

Armed Forces Day
1 October
Military parades are often held in Seoul on this day.

National Foundation Day, National Holiday
3 October
Called Kae Chun Chul in Korean, this day's literal translation is Sky Opening Day. This commemorates the day in 2333 BC when legendary Tan-gun founded the Korean race.

Hangul Day
9 October
This day celebrates the creation in 1446 of *hangul*, the phonetic Korean alphabet that gave the race its literacy. Until that time, there were only the difficult Chinese characters which no one but the elite scholars could read.

Christmas Day, National Holiday
25 December

Christmas is very visible throughout Korea, with Christmas lights and decorations in the market, decorated trees in many coffee shops and hotels and bargain sales at the major department stores. For the sizeable Christian population in Korea, as for Christians everywhere, this is a religious holiday. For the others, it is another excuse to get together with friends for drinks.

Surviving Christmas

For the expatriate who is unable to go home for Christmas, this holiday can be a lonely time. Separated from loved ones, no quantity of tinsel, greeting cards or Santa Clauses can create that familiar spirit. Certainly, the parties and programmes organised by Korean and foreign organisations do not appear to fill this gap.

Many expatriates have found it more helpful to start new traditions than cling to the old ones. Santa Claus can never get into a 13th floor flat with a guard and no chimney. Getting together with other westerners, making some non-traditional but special food and observing those customs that are transferable to Korea are excellent ways to build memories in a foreign land. Several churches offer special services in English, and even at the Korean churches you will be able to hear the familiar Christmas melodies.

Official Holidays

New Year's Day	1 January
Seollal	January–February
Independence Movement Day	1 March
Arbor Day	5 April
Buddha's Birthday	April–May
Children's Day	5 May
Memorial Day	6 June
Constitution Day	17 July
Liberation Day	15 August
Chuseok	September–October
National Foundation Day	3 October
Christmas	25 December

TRADITIONAL FOLK GAMES

Department stores and the *moon bang goo* (a kind of Korean stationery store) sell modern toys and games, but these are newcomers to the Korean home. Most Koreans over 40 had few if any toys when they were children. Still, they had lots of fun, as many do even today, playing traditional Korean games such as *yoot, paduk, changgi* and *nul ddwee gee*.

Yoot Or Yunnori

This game is particularly popular on New Year's Day. There are four sticks, rounded on one side and flat on the other. The players are divided into two teams, and take turns throwing

Men enjoying a pick-up game of Yoot.

the sticks into the air. If they land with one side flat and three round, one point is awarded the team. If the result is two flat, two round, then two points. Three points are given for three flat and one round and four points for all flat. The maximum of five points is given to the team with all rounded sides up. The teams advance a marker around a circle, and the first team to finish wins.

Part of the fun in playing this game is the yelling and cheering. Every time the sticks are thrown, one team or another offers loud encouragement. The food and alcohol thoughtfully provided by the hostess add to the fun and noise level. When this game is played, it does not go unnoticed by neighbours.

As Koreans find it hard to explain the game to the foreigner, they are likely to encourage him to throw the sticks just like the other players. No matter what the result, they will tell him he has great skill, and he is likely to believe them, not knowing exactly what skill is required. In any case, it is a lot of fun for people of all ages.

Baduk

This game is especially popular among men. It is played on a wooden board that has squares drawn on it. Small markers are placed at the intersections of the lines. One player has black markers, the other white. The goal of the game is to surround the other player's pieces. Strategies to achieve the object can be very complex and many educated people spend hours each week playing *paduk*. Games played by nationally recognised players are sometimes televised. *Paduk* requires great concentration, strategy and a lot of time and is more complex than chess. In Japan it is called *go*.

Janggi

This game is similar to chess. Each player has 16 pieces, of seven different types. They are placed on a board with ten horizontal and nine vertical lines. The player who immobilises his opponent's pieces wins the game. The board and pieces are made in a variety of sizes, and portable versions are often taken along on picnics.

Neolttwigi (Seesaw)

This Korean see-saw is different from western see-saws, and is particularly popular among women. A long board is balanced on a bag filled with rice straw. The participants stand on each end. One jumps into the air and lands on the board, sending the other flying. It takes skill to time a jump to co-ordinate with a partner's landing.

The game was especially popular during the Yi dynasty, when women were confined inside the high walls surrounding their property. As they leapt high into the air, they hoped to catch a glimpse of the outside world. It was also a good form of exercise, for women could not go outside. One is not likely to see this game played much in cities, but at the Folk Village, south of Seoul, visitors may try the *neolttwigi*.

Kite Flying

On the lunar New Year, which often falls in February, boys like to fly kites. Korean kites are usually white with a design of red, blue and yellow painted on them, and they very often have a large hole in the middle. They are flown by holding the string wrapped around a reel made with four sticks.

Sometimes the fliers glue glass dust on the string, and try to approach other kites in mid-air in order to cut their strings. Traditionally, on the last day of the first moon, people would

A human national treasure performing a traditional Korean tightrope walk at the Korean Folk Village.

write 'Away Evil, Come Blessings' on their kites and release them, fondly believing that their families' bad luck would fly away with the kite.

Swinging

The Korean swing was traditionally used primarily by women. The swing was hung from a tall tree or a special stand next to thick ropes. Players would stand up on the swing. This was an especially popular game during holidays. Expatriates can also try this at the Folk Village at Suwon, to the south of Seoul.

Shi–Reum

Shi-reum is a unique form of Korean wrestling. Each participant binds his right leg tightly with a long cloth. He grabs his opponent's thigh with his right hand, and the end of the cloth with his left hand, then the participants face each other in a semi-squatting position. To win, one player must force the other to lose his balance so that his body touches the ground. This game is always played in a sand pit.

Hwatu (Cards)

This Korean card game consists of heavy, small cards featuring flowers which represent the different seasons of the year. It is played with much enthusiasm as the cards are slapped down on the table.

TRAVEL AROUND KOREA

Since Korea is a small country, it is easy to get to the many regional attractions located throughout the peninsula. One can drive, take a bus or train to any of these places.

Gyeonju

The capital of the Shilla Kingdom, Gyeonju is a popular destination to Koreans and foreigners alike. It is actually a cluster of many historical remains, designated by UNESCO as one of the 10 major historical sites in the world. The Shilla kingdom is know for it's artistic treasures, some of which can be seen at the Gyeongu National Museum: metal work, paintings, calligraphy, carved jade and earthenware. Most famous is Pulguksa, a well-known and beautiful temple. East of Gyeonju is Pomun Lake, with international hotels, a golf course, pleasure boats and an amusement park.

Sorak-san National Park

A popular hiking destination, this national park on the east coast can also be explored by taking a cable car to the top. Nestled close to the rugged, rocky mountains is the eastern sea. The public beach, Naksan, can be enjoyed by all. First class hotels are scattered throughout this region, making it a great short getaway for people who yearn to be surrounded by nature's beauty. Two natural hot springs are in the vicinity. Sorak-san is especially popular in the autumn, when the maple leaves are blazing and the air is crisp and clear.

Jeju-do

An island off the south-west coast of Korea, Jeju-do offers a climate and culture markedly different from the rest of Korea. A favourite honeymoon spot, this island, formed by a volcanic eruption, features white sandy beaches, forested areas and green rice fields; Jeju-do is renowned for these things. Traditionally, women divers would gather seaweed and shellfish, while their husbands cared for the home. Because of its tropical climate, Jeju can also grow delicious mandarin oranges, enjoyed throughout Korea during the winter. World class hotels and golf courses have been built to accommodate people wanting to enjoy the beauty of this unique island.

Pammujom and the Dmilitarised Zone (DMZ)

Located 40 km (25 miles) north of Seoul, Pammujom is where the 1953 Armistice was signed but the realisation that a war could break out at any time is palpable at the DMZ. Security is high and the mood is solemn in this 4 km (2.5 mile) wide, 250 km (155.3 mile) long line that divides North and South Korea. Visitors can see tall North Korean soldiers up close.

Hein-sa

Korea's largest temple is located in the Gaya Mountains in south Gyeongsang Province. As all temples in provincial Korea, Hein-sa is situated in a gorgeous setting, surrounded by mountains and forests. Hein-sa houses the Tripitaka Koreana, a collection of more than 80,000 woodblocks with Buddhist scriptures and is designated a Unesco World Heritage Site. Hein-sa is known for wild dried mushrooms and the restaurant menus in the area feature this fungus delicacy. Ample, uncrowded trails beckon even the most reluctant hiker to higher views.

Hot Springs

Since Koreans appreciate the relaxation and health benefits of natural hot springs, it is unsurprising that these areas have become tourist destinations. Expatriates living in Korea also enjoy going to the many hot springs scattered throughout the country. An hour from Seoul is Icheon Hotspring, which is also home to a ceramics village and museum. In the Chunungcheong Province area are the Onynag Hot Springs, the Asan Hot Springs and the Suanbo Hot Springs. For families, Bugok Hot Spings in Gyeongsang Province is a popular destination because of the numerous pools and water activities for people of all ages.

INTERNATIONAL TRAVEL WHILE LIVING IN KOREA

Since Korea is centrally located, most expatriates living in Korea take advantage of their close proximity to other Pacific Ocean countries. Beijing, the ancient and now-bustling capital of China, is just a two hour plane ride from Seoul and parts of Japan are even closer. Hong Kong, long known as an international shopping hub, is equally accessible. For destinations closer to nature and warm all year round, Korean-based expatriates can travel to Vietnam, Cambodia, Thailand and Malaysia. While Australia and New Zealand are a long flight from Korea, they are likely to be closer to Korea than they are be from most expatriates home countries.

ACTIVITIES TO PURSUE WHILE LIVING IN KOREA

Expatriates in Korea can pursue most of their favourite activities while living in the country. It's also possible that once you are outside your familiar environment, you may decide to develop some new interests. Golf has long been popular among business people and, with the success of Mi Hyun Kim, Seri Park and Grace Park, the sport's popularity has spread. Driving ranges are located in major cities and golf courses, though quite expensive, are accessible throughout Korea. Skiing has become another popular pastime, with lifts open from December to early March. Active sports enthusiasts can enjoy rafting, water skiing, wind surfing and scuba diving, horseback riding and cycling. Hiking is another wonderful way to explore the natural beauty of Korea and many nature parks and other hiking trails are located within and outside of cities. For children and those young at heart, Korea is home to numerous amusement parks, primarily in the Seoul vicinity. Seoul Land, Everland and Lotte World feature rides and other fun for children whilst the outskirts of Seoul also boasts an impressive zoo.

This Korean calligrapher at the Folk Village can draw your name.

Short or long term visitors to Korea should not miss the Korean Folk Village, a living museum which provides a glimpse into traditional Korean culture. It is located east of Suwon, about an hour south of Seoul. Artisans, dressed in period clothes, demonstrate pottery-making, basket-weaving and blacksmithing. There are 260 homes representing different regions of Korea at different time periods. A market portrays traditional Korean crafts and traditional foods and several times each day, performances of Korean folk dances take place, including the mask dance and the fan dance. Drumming is also held for visitors to enjoy. In th short space of several hours, one has a through introduction to Korean culture.

Given Korea's 5,000-year-old history and the pride that Korean's have in their culture, it is not surprising that there are museums and art galleries located across the peninsula to preserve and display Korea's rich heritage. Seoul houses the National Musuem of Korea, the National Folk Museum, Seoul Metropolitan Museum of Art and the Olympic Park Outdoor Sculpture Garden and the Sejong Cultural Centre. The Korean National Tourist Organisation provides helpful information on these and many others. There are also numerous traditional and modern performance theatres, featuring world class dance, theatre and music performances.

Expanding Your Horizons

Expatriates in Korea have enjoyed learning about traditional Korean arts such as dance, pottery, textiles or listening to or playing traditional Korean instruments. Others have learned or improved their martial arts skills in Taekwondo or Hapkido and in addition, expatriates can take formal or informal Korean cooking classes.

Volunteer activities also abound. English teachers living away from major cities often spend time at orphanages, playing with the children. One can volunteer at the Seoul Help Centre for Foreigners if one lives in Seoul, with working people's groups, women's organisations, churches and schools being other venues for volunteering.

PUBLIC BATHS

It would be a shame to live in Korea and not experience a popular activity of Koreans: the public bath. Traditionally, homes did not have bathing facilities and family members would go to the public bath regularly. Children accompanied their mothers in gender segregated facilities, until their sons became old enough to go on the men's side. The traditional bath, called a *mogyoktang*, has clear rules. Today, most homes and flats are equipped with baths and showers but Koreans still enjoy going to the public variety.

To begin, one must bath before entering the hot bath so as to keep the common bath area clean. There are faucets placed about waist-high for the purpose of washing and after soaking in warm water, it is common to get scrubbed with a very rough cloth, specially made for this purpose. This sheds the dead skin loosened up in the soaking. Since going to the public bath is a social event, normally friends or family members scrub one another but sometimes a bath attendant offers to do this. After the scrub, one must again rinse off in the low faucet. A more recent development that has quickly become a favourite activity for families, couples and friends is the *jimjilbang* which includes a sauna and private places for small groups of people to relax. Refreshments are also available. To participate in either of these relaxing and uniquely Korean activities you will need to shed your modesty (only among people of the same gender). If you don't speak Korean, is best to let a Korean friend of the same gender guide you through the process.

COMMUNICATING

CHAPTER 8

'It's more in how you say it than in what you say.'
—A Korean Proverb

THE LANGUAGE

Being able to communicate with those around you is essential and yet expatriates moving to Korea recognise what a formidable obstacle this is. Koreans not only have their own grammar and vocabulary, they have their own alphabet. And unlike Hong Kong, Paris or Oslo, one cannot easily manage daily living in Korea with English. While all Koreans have studied English in school, many cannot communicate well in person with an English-speaking person.

Nevertheless, learning to communicate in Korea has some redeeming features. Firstly, learning any Korean, even the equivalents of 'hello', 'thank you' and 'how much does this cost' will be received with great appreciation. Koreans recognise how difficult their language is for others to learn and their faces are likely to light up when they hear foreigners say something in Korean. Your efforts to learn even a few words will be well rewarded in smiles and, sometimes, lower prices. This is true even when speaking with Koreans who are fluent in English. The one exception to the rule is levelled at people of Korean ancestry, whether adopted or raised abroad. In some cases but not all, Koreans may be critical that one's parents didn't teach them the Korean language (even if those parents were Swedish).

Secondly, the Korean writing system, *hangul,* is simple to learn. Compared to languages that use pictorial representation of words, such as Chinese and Japanese which take years to master, *hangul* can be readily learned. It generally takes less than four hours to memorise the 24 phonetic symbols. *hangul* is a simple, scientific and phonetic alphabet consisting of 10 vowels, 11 vowel blends and 14 consonants which form syllables. With a handful of exceptions, one sound is represented by one symbol and one symbol can be pronounced only one way. Those having trouble spelling in English will be able to spell perfectly in Korean. Though at first *hangul* seems incomprehensible, it can be learned by adults and children alike. Once learned, the expatriate can read everything, though understanding what the sounds mean is another matter. Since many English words are written in *hangul*, it is not unusual to sound out a *hangul* word and realise that one is actually reading a familiar English word. Since *hangul* is so painless to learn, it makes sense to learn it before learning the spoken language. Even if one is not planning to learn the language, learning the alphabet makes the environment seem more familiar and can be fun. Sounding out *hangul* words is reminiscent of learning to read in one's native language, so many years ago.

And thirdly, living or spending considerable time in Korea is the ideal environment for learning a new language. Every new word one learns will make one's life simpler. There are language experts everywhere you turn, willing to give you the name for the things you point to. Also, hearing the language on a daily basis makes it easier to learn the correct pronunciation and many expatriates who know only a handful of Korean expressions find that they spread goodwill and joy wherever they use them.

Background of the Korean Language

The Korean language is a member of the Altaic family and shares similarities with the Mongolian and Manchurian languages. Linguists also point out grammatical similarities between Korean, Finnish and Japanese, with the verb being always placed at the end of the sentence. Initially, Chinese characters were used by scholars in Korea, but in 1446, King Sejong invented *hangul*, the Korean alphabet, so that all Koreans could learn to read. About 1800 Chinese characters are still used in Korea and can be seen on name cards, in newspapers and on a few store signs.

Regional accents exist in Korea, such that people from Seoul, the southeast and the southwest can be distinguished by their speech. Elderly people who spent their formative years in North Korea, as well as newly arrived refugees from the North, also speak in an identifiable way. Seoulites consider their speech standard and expatriates living in the outer provinces have been warned that they will not learn proper Korean if they learn to speak in another dialect. People throughout South Korea have no problem understanding one another. Since 1945, the Korean language has developed independently in North and South Korea, causing minor difficulties for people from these two countries to communicate with one another today.

Not surprisingly, Koreans communicate respect and closeness to others through their language. Older or higher positioned persons use informal verb forms when speaking to their subordinates. When highly positioned people speak to one another in the language children use, one knows they have been close friends since childhood. Children learn the simplest and least formal language first and as they become older they learn to use more respectful language to the appropriate people. When one learns Korean as an adult, one begins by learning the more respectful verb forms, which is also more difficult, but avoids insulting people by using too familiar language. In the early stages of learning Korean, one may be confused by the different forms of the same word (including the words for 'hello' and 'goodbye') but these can be readily learned when one is surrounded by the language.

English can often be heard sprinkled within Korean conversation—words such as 'computer', 'supermarket', 'aspirin' and 'bus'. Many new and/or scientific foreign terms have also been adopted. There is no hostility to employing such foreign words, and there may even be some special status associated with these words. Many products advertised on Korean television have English product names. When communicating with Koreans, it is important to use their pronunciation for these words, not the original pronunciation that you are familiar with, or you will not be understood. For example, coffee, computer and even Pizza Hut may not be understood unless one uses the Korean pronunciation.

A mistake that expatriates often make when speaking Korean is mispronouncing a vowel. This is particularly true if one is speaking from romanised spellings of Korean words. Korea has fewer sounds than many languages and the slight distinction between vowels is important to observe or one will be saying a different word and be misunderstood by a Korean listeners. It may seem picky or puzzling to the expatriate but getting the vowel sound exactly right it critical in many cases. The multiple sounds that are represented in English by the letter 'o' in particular, need to be distinguished.

Romanising Korean words is difficult. The Korean government has recently standardised how particular Korean sounds are romanised but the older phonetic forms still exist. One can find several different romanisations of Korean words making place names especially problematic. Chamsil, Chamshil and Jamshil all refer to the same place. This is yet another reason to learn *hangul* as the spelling of places and other words will be consistent and accurate.

Learning the Korean Language

There are many approaches to learning Korean, whether one's goal is to learn a bit or become fluent. Personal factors such as one's purpose for being in Korea, one's access to translators, one's desire and aptitude for learning another language, one's learning style and the time one has to devote to language learning influence the ways expatriates go about learning Korean.

Several language institutes exist at major Seoul universities such as Yonsei, Ewha and Sogang, where one can study Korean every day or less frequently for periods as short as 10 weeks. Those needing to be fluent in Korean may continue intensive study for more than a year whilst those wanting to use it to facilitate daily life may do well to study Korean for one ten-week session to develop a basic foundation. Even a short course can teach one enough to manage basic

HANGUL

CONSONANTS

Letter	Pronunciation	Letter	Pronunciation
ㄱ	g	ㅇ	ng
ㄴ	n	ㅈ	j
ㄷ	d	ㅊ	ch
ㄹ	r	ㅋ	k
ㅁ	m	ㅌ	t
ㅂ	b	ㅍ	p
ㅅ	s	ㅎ	h

VOWELS

Letter	Pronunciation
ㅏ	ah
ㅑ	ya
ㅓ	o (as in dog)
ㅕ	yaw
ㅗ	oh
ㅛ	yo (as in yo-yo)
ㅜ	u (as in blue)
ㅠ	you
—	oo (as in good)
ㅣ	ee (as in see)
ㅐ	a (as in mat)

VOWEL BLENDS

Letter	Pronunciation
ㅒ	ye (as in yeah)
ㅔ	aye
ㅖ	ye (as in yellow)
ㅚ	way
ㅘ	wa (as in water)
ㅝ	wo (as in won)
ㅙ	wea (as in weather)
ㅞ	wei (as in weight)
ㅟ	wee
ㅢ	eui

Examples of syllables with vertical vowels (first consonant is placed to the left of the vowel, the last below the vowel):

Hangul	Pronunciation	Meaning
밤	bahm	night
말	mahl	horse
선	sun	line

Examples of syllables with horizontal vowels (first consonant is placed above the vowel, the last below the vowel)

Hangul	Pronunciation	Meaning
눈	noon	eye
문	moon	door
불	bool	fire

speaking with confidence. Further learning will take place as one goes about daily life. English language newspapers in Korea are a good source of Korean language programmes but be aware that one is unlikely to find a Korean language institute outside major Korean cities.

Private Korean lessons, either individually or in a small group, is another way to learn the language and fits better into some people's schedules; some husbands and wives learn together several evenings a week after the working spouse returns home. Language institutes and other expatriates would be a good place to find skilled Korean language tutors.

Since Korea could be said to be 'mad about English', another option, particularly for those without much discretionary income, it to trade English lessons for Korean lessons. The quality of the learning would depend on how qualified both participants are in explaining their own language to another person as speaking a language does not necessarily qualify one for teaching it.

WORKING AND DOING BUSINESS

CHAPTER 9

'With single-minded devotion,
anything can be achieved in this world.'
—A Korean Proverb

IN 1963, SOUTH KOREA'S PER CAPITA GROSS NATIONAL PRODUCT stood at US$ 100, one of the lowest in the world. This densely populated country with few natural resources was just beginning to rebuild itself after the Korean War. In 2004, the per capita GNP exceeded US$ 14,000, a remarkable increase in just 40 years. Today, South Korea has the 11th largest economy in the world. Along with this impressive economic development have come numerous opportunities for foreigners to come to Korea to work in Korean companies, to teach English and to manage Korean branches of foreign corporations.

The purpose of this chapter is to help you with the cultural aspects of working in Korean. Information is provided to help you avoid some of the likely pitfalls as well as give you an understanding of how Korean organisations operate. Even a basic understanding of some of the unique aspects of the Korean work environment can make an important difference in the success of your efforts and the satisfaction you gain from your work. That said, challenges await each expatriate working in Korea. Since work revolves around relationships, this will be addressed first, followed by a discussion of the hierarchical structure of Korean organisations. Communication and loyalty in the workplace will be examined, as will workplace etiquette. The chapter will end by addressing particular work situations expatriates might experience in Korea.

MAKING RELATIONSHIPS A PRIORITY

One cannot overestimate the importance of developing good relationships with work associates in Korea. While Koreans also want a successful organisation or profitable business, they place greater importance on the people doing the work and on the nature of their relationships. To westerners who are accustomed to an efficient and logical approach, this stress on interpersonal relationships and group harmony is excessive. Positive working relationships require time (both short and long term), money, honesty and care. Being mindful of the value of developing and maintaining positive personal relationships with work associates will set one off on a good course of work. These relationships also have the potential to enrich one's life, foster personal and cross-cultural understanding, and facilitate successful organisations or businesses. The relationships one develops with Koreans at work will also facilitate adjustments to other aspects of Korean life, since co-workers are likely to be the people you turn to when you need help finding things or navigating puzzling aspects of Korea.

While to some expatriates the emphasis Koreans place on workplace relationships can be burdensome, many are equally impressed with the sense of connection and caring Korean workers have for one another, and for you. It is not unusual, for example, for teachers to contribute a set percentage of their salary to a community fund that is used for going out to lunch together periodically or to help a colleague undergoing a difficult situation (e.g. family death). Events important to one worker are acknowledged and often celebrated by others. A person may provide treats and drinks for co-workers when she or he buys a new car or house and your membership in a workplace automatically makes you important to your co-workers.

Developing Good Relationships with Work Associates

As important as relationships are to the life of Korean workers, one would be correct in assuming that this is not a quick and simple thing. Fortunately, most Koreans at your workplace are looking to develop a good relationship with you, recognising that their relationship with you will also benefit them. Koreans will take care to introduce you to the people in your work setting that you need to know and you will no doubt be taken out to eat and drink, giving you the opportunity to get to know your work associates on a personal level. These socialising experiences are an excellent opportunity for them to know you better.

One of the best ways to begin a relationship is to look for things you have in common, such as hobbies, travel experiences, past residences and current social activities. The more fun people have together, the more connected and comfortable they feel. During these early social activities, your Korean work associates will be watching you carefully, trying to determine if you are of good character, flexible, sensitive to other people and willing to share yourself with them. They will observe your attitude about Korea and Koreans and you will certainly be asked about your impressions of their country. Note that your answers should include only things you like about Korea until you have known someone for a long time and have a close and open relationship. In addition, you will likely be asked personal questions that may seem intrusive but the purpose is to get to know you better and to find out areas of mutual interest. While you do not have to answer questions you are uncomfortable answering, keeping all your thoughts and experiences to yourself will not be in your best interest. Though at first you will be invited out at your colleagues' expense, don't forget that you will be expected to return the favour before too much time has passed.

Having Fun with Your Work Associates

One of the best ways to develop good relationships with Korean co-workers, bosses and subordinates is to have fun together. Activities such as hiking, tennis or visiting cultural sites are quite common for Korea workers to do together. You would be wise to participate in these events as a way to get to know your colleagues. Compared to the past, younger workers in Korea are not as willing to spend evenings and weekends with their co-workers but nevertheless, to expatriates, the amount of time work associates spend with one another, inside and outside of work, is likely to seem excessive.

Being Yourself in Your Relationships

While Koreans highly value harmony and are sensitive to one another, they also appreciate and expect individuality and are likely to appreciate and enjoy your idiosyncrasies. Expatriates in Korea soon notice the different personalities in their co-workers. It is important also to observe the general principles of Korean etiquette, including respect for positions and hierarchy, but beyond that, expatriates of all personalities have been warmly welcomed into Korean organisations. As a foreigner, you are not expected to fully follow all of the Korean rules and your oddities may very well be celebrated as long as it is clear that you make your relationship with your co-workers a priority.

Nurturing Work Relationships

After attending numerous dinners and parties with one's work associates, the expatriate may, in the first month, come to the conclusion that the relationships are built and one can finally have time to oneself. This would be an incorrect assumption. Work relationships need to be nurtured over the course of one's employment. Invitations are usually made at the last minute yet Koreans normally are able to arrange to join in. Co-workers socialise on a regular basis and rejecting these opportunities frequently reflects badly on an expatriate worker. Participating in these events, on the other hand, makes you part of your work group and allows work activities to proceed smoothly. Korean colleagues' confidence in you will be enhanced.

Similarly, if one leaves Korea but may one day need to work with Korean associates again, it is wise to keep connected through occasional emails, holiday cards or phone calls. Should one need something from Korea in the future, it will be much easier if one has maintained a relationships over the years. Likewise, the goodwill you have generated between your company and individual Koreans will provide important benefits to your organisation. Should your relationship with co-workers be negative, that too will be reflected in future relationships between your companies. Beyond the utilitarian value of relationships with Koreans, many expatriates have enjoyed lifelong, close relationships with their former Korean co-workers.

OBSERVING HEIRARCHY AND RECOGNISING POSITIONS AND TITLES

Korean society is based on a Confucian hierarchical social system in which Koreans need to know the position of another person in order to determine how to relate to him, whether in terms of respect given or the language to use in conversation. Korean companies are part of this social system and individual identities are closely tied to the positions they hold within a given organisation. For this reason, knowing the position of a person in a Korean company is significant when one interacts with him. People in their late forties and older are more sensitive to position and hierarchy whereas younger Koreans are less concerned with hierarchy.

A clue to the importance of position lies in the way Koreans address each other. They would never call President Kim, Mr Kim. Nor would they use his personal name. Managing Director Park is addressed as such, never as Mr Park or by his personal name. Koreans are familiar with the western way of calling people by their personal names, or by the usual honorarium of 'Mr', as in Mr Smith, instead of Director Smith. But they would appreciate your efforts to call them as they call each other—by their titles. Furthermore, using the title not only gives each Korean his due respect, it helps the foreigner distinguish between the multitude of Mr Kims, Mr Parks and Mr Lees.

Titles of Key Positions

- **Hwoe Jang**   Chairman
- **Sa Jang**   President
- **Bu Sa Jang**   VP
- **Sang Moo Ee Sa**   Director

- **Cha Jang**   Manager
- **Kwa Jang**   Section Manager
- **Dae Ri**   Assistant Manager
- **Kay Jang**   Supervisor

When addressing someone of equal or higher status than yourself, you should add the honorific *nim* at the end of a name. For example, President Kim should be addressed or referred to as Kim Sa Jang Nim.

Principles, presidents, supervisors and managers tend to have more power over their subordinates than they might have in a similar western organisation. So ingrained is Confucian respect for seniors, that it is difficult for a Korean to criticise or go against what his senior thinks or wants. Those occupying lower positions have little choice but to follow their seniors' directions. It is also difficult for someone of lower status to inform a superior that something is wrong.

Though Koreans are moving towards more merit promotions, in the past, workers were promoted based on age, not on work performance. This allowed everyone to maintain face and minimises awkward interactions. It is quite possible that a younger western worker, who has advanced quickly, will be supervising older Koreans. This is a strange situation for Koreans. Nevertheless, it is easier for them to be supervised by a younger expatriate than by a Korean of that same age. Expatriates do not fit into the hierarchy quite as neatly and this gives the expatriate flexibility.

Presidents, especially those in larger organisations, have learnt to delegate responsibility. So while it is nice to be introduced to people in high positions, they will sometimes know little about your particular project, and will refer you to the appropriate person. Presidents and supervisors will often trust dependable subordinates, so it is important not to offend or neglect the lower ranks.

Generally, people of similar positions in different organisations work with one another. If you have a high position in your organisation, and a person of noticeably lower status acts as the representative of his company when relating to you, you can assume that the company is not particularly interested in what yours has to offer.

Treatment towards Superiors

- Use honorific language, plus the most complimentary title
- Bow first, a bit slower and lower
- Let your superior eat first
- Pour drinks for them first
- Use your right hand and, to be most respectful, both hands for pouring drinks and handing objects
- Show concern for his/her physical health
- Compliment when warranted
- Offer to help/be a gofer
- Defer to his/her decisions
- Be sensitive towards superior's moods
- Punctuality is important
- Traditionally one did not leave the office until their superior had left

Treatment towards Subordinates

- Use familiar language
- Ask them to do things for you
- Pay for food/beverages (in most cases)
- Introduce them to jobs, contacts
- Give helpful advice
- Rarely thank/compliment
- Accept responsibility for subordinate's errors

Treatment towards Equals

- Use polite language unless you are on very familiar terms
- Reciprocate favours
- Reciprocate paying
- Socialise frequently
- Thank/compliment infrequently
- Be sensitive towards other person's mood/feeling

COMMUNICATION IN THE WORKPLACE

Communicating effectively is a prerequisite to being a successful worker or conducting a successful business in any country. It can be a difficult skill to master when working in the country.

Introductions

In Korea, when you wish to begin a business relationship with someone, it is very important to be introduced to that person by a third party. Contacting an unknown person directly without going through an intermediary is viewed with suspicion.

Due to the significance of introductions, it is easy to see why you should maintain as wide a social network as possible. Fortunately, since South Korea is a small society, it is not as difficult as you might think to be introduced to people you wish to meet. Alumni can also freely contact each other, even though they have not been formally introduced, as can members of the same social or business association. Consequently, joining various organisations, even organisations for expatriates, will be a source for these important networking connections.

If you know who you wish to approach, you can ask the people you do know to introduce you to that person. Even when they are unable to help you, they may introduce you to someone else who can, in turn, introduce you.

Tips for Greeting Someone for the First Time
- Stand up for greetings
- Shake hands (not too hard or firm)
- Bow (not as deep or long as Japanese)
- Say '*Ban gop sumnida*' (I'm happy to meet you)

Name Cards

Name cards are essential to workers in Korea. When two people meet before they even fully rise from their bow they exchange name cards. Each person looks carefully at the other person's card which identifies the person's position and, likely, the relative status of each party. The name card of another person is treated with care, not stuffed in a pocket or set on a table. These cards come in very handy when one cannot remember a person's name or when one wants to make contact with that person. Expatriates, like Koreans, usually have one side of the card printed in Korean, the other in English. Cards made of thin cardstock or poor-quality printing does not reflect favourably on the owner.

Tips for exchanging business cards

- Exchange is a ritualised and important part of first meeting which lets everyone know where they stand
- Cards are exchanged while you are standing
- Cards are presented and received with both hands, with the writing on the card facing the receiver
- Upon receipt, study the other person's card for a moment
- Place it in front of you on the table
- Take care of the card (don't treat it as a scrap of paper or a bookmark and keep it for future reference)

LANGUAGE

Though many expatriates find that Koreans are more proficient in English than people from other Asian-speaking countries, there are still barriers to good verbal communication. While all educated Koreans have studied English in primary school, secondary school and college, many have had little experience communicating verbally: the emphasis has been on reading and writing. Until recently, speaking and listening skills, so different from those used in reading and writing, have not been taught. Many Koreans may have difficulty understanding you and expressing their own ideas in English. And often when they don't understand, they pretend that they do.

At first, you may overestimate the abilities of your Korean co-workers. To facilitate verbal communication keep the following in mind:

- Speak patiently and slowly.
- Repeat key points several times, or write them down.
- If speaking to two Koreans, pause occasionally so that one may translate for the other, or to allow them to discuss with each other (in Korean) what they think you are saying.
- Find a tactful way of asking the listener to paraphrase what you said.

- When negotiating, you may want to have your own translator with you.

Many experienced expatriate workers in Korea stress the importance of learning some Korean. This will endear you to your Korean partners. It is probably unrealistic to expect anyone who plans to live in Korea for two to three years to learn to speak the language fluently; it is sensible, however, to learn several useful expressions.

THE MEANING OF 'YES'

In English, 'yes' usually means 'I agree' or 'I will do it'. The Korean 'yes' means 'I understand' or 'I'll do my best'. It is important you understand exactly what someone when they say 'yes'.

A related issue is the way negative questions are answered differently in the Korean and English language. "You're

Tips for Business Conversation

- Personalise relationships (hobbies, travels, interests)
- Make efforts to make everyone comfortable
- Humility is admired
- Don't talk much about your own or others' family
- Don't compare Korea negatively to Japan
- Don't criticise Korea
- Do try to ask questions about customs in a very non-judgmental way
- Don't interrupt
- Note that a speaker may continue for a lengthy time, especially if he/she is highly ranked
- Silence is okay
- Avoid the use of slang and idioms (these may not be readily understood)
- Be sensitive to negative questions "You're not going?" "Yes, I'm not going."
- Direct negative communication is avoided. "Yes." may mean, "Yes, I understand."

not coming with?" would be responded in English "No" meaning "No, I'm not going with." A Korean with the same intention may answer "Yes", meaning "Yes, I'm not going with." Koreans respond by agreeing or disagreeing with the speaker whereas English speakers agree or disagree with the statement. Another example is how one would respond to "You're not married are you?" An English speaker might say "No" meaning "No, I'm not married" but a Korean speaker might say "Yes" meaning "Yes, I'm not married". For this reason it is best to avoid negative questions.

RECOGNISING THE KOREAN 'NO'

This impolite (to the Korean) word is seldom heard in a Korean work environment. A Korean would say 'no' indirectly. A Korean banker put it thus: "Rather than saying I won't make a loan, I make the loan conditions so unfavourable that it could not possibly be accepted."

Sometimes a Korean may agree to do something, but later you find it is not done. His intention is not to deceive you. He may have meant, 'If it is possible, I will do it', then later discovered he could not. When a promise to do something keeps being put off, he may be indirectly saying 'no'. Also, someone may agree to do something, such as go to dinner, even when he doesn't intend to do so, to avoid making you uncomfortable.

USE OF THE TELEPHONE

Important work communication by telephone is not the norm in Korea. The telephone is used to make appointments, or to confirm details, but most communication occurs face to face. Direct personal contact also tends to strengthen the personal relationship between the two parties. Koreans sometimes end phone conversations in a way that seems abrupt to foreigners, hanging up when they have finished talking without saying goodbye.

NON-VERBAL COMMUNICATION

Besides the non-verbal ways of communicating discussed in Chapter Four, there are rules specific to the workplace.

Workplace Dress

Koreans place a high value on appearance and this is true in the workplace, too. Dress is a reflection of one's character and one's status and it also demonstrates respect to those one is meeting. Expatriates in Korea may find that Koreans dress more formally than those in their home country. It is best to err on the side of conservative. For businessmen, a tie is always necessary, and when you leave the office a suit jacket should be worn. Women should dress professionally.

THE EMBARASSED SMILE

You may also encounter difficulty in correctly interpreting a Korean's smile. Besides being an expression of happiness, a smile can mean shame or embarrassment. When your assistant mistakenly erases several hours of your work on the computer, he is most likely to smile, or even laugh. This does not mean that he finds the situation funny. It means that he is embarrassed and sorry. You will quickly learn to read the smile by the particular context.

Deadlines

When a Korean agrees to do something within a time frame, he generally says 'about this time'. This gives all parties concerned some leniency in case the unexpected happens. After all, the two parties trust each other, and each must assume that the other party will do his best. Only a reason beyond his control would prevent a person from meeting a deadline. Showing anger in the face of a late project is, in effect, to doubt the good intentions of the responsible party.

Business Contracts

While contracts often form the basis of business deals in South Korea as in the west, the nature of such agreements is often significantly different.

The Meaning Of Contracts

Misunderstandings often arise over the issue of contracts. While most of the large international South Korean companies have learnt the meaning of contracts, companies less accustomed to international business may not have. The problem is that Koreans and westerners view contracts differently. To some Koreans, a contract is merely a general guide for conducting business. It is assumed that after agreements are signed, concessions will be made. A change in conditions, some Koreans assume, may invalidate the details of a particular contract and for them, a contract is not as important as the interpersonal relationship between the two parties. A contract made between two people who do not trust each other has little value. Fortunately, an increasing number of Koreans now recognise that contracts are legally binding but it is still necessary to be aware of the other view.

Workers in Korea would be wise to not only check the contract they are signing very carefully, but find out as much as you can about the company and/or individual making the contract. Do not hesitate to insist that certain things be put in our taken out of the agreement, even if they seem minor. For example, though you are told that appliances will be included in the furnished flat, ask that those appliances be clearly written in the contract. English language institutes are notorious for taking advantage of, and not fully meeting, promises associated with their western employees. Whenever possible, make contact with others who had worked for the same organisation to find out about their experiences there.

Reaching an Agreement in Business Contracts

The politeness and gentleness many Korean businessmen exhibit may fool you into thinking that they are pushovers in the negotiating process. Actually, Koreans lead very competitive lives, beginning in primary school, through to the university entrance examination, right up to competing for a position in their company. They hold their own at the negotiating table. Remember that a good relationship continues to be important as one negotiates contracts so socialising is an efficient use of time and money in business dealings, even if no business is addressed during your social encounter.

You will need to be firm about your position, remembering two things: insisting on having your way, with no flexibility, will be viewed unfavourably by your Korean counterparts; and appearing to be in a hurry puts you at a disadvantage. Not revealing your departure date could work to your advantage. Koreans may pressure you to accept less than ideal terms just to finalise an agreement before you leave. Being flexible does not imply giving in to demands that you consider totally unreasonable.

Koreans prefer to reach a general agreement, leaving sticky details to be worked out later, perhaps by subordinates in the two companies. In fact, they would prefer not to be too specific in the contract, but to allow flexibility for both parties. Often, contracts are made verbally, in a social context, and written up formally in the office later.

Once the contract has been written up, it may take time to get the final approval. Sometimes several government agencies need to be involved, each with its own process of red tape.

LOYALTY IN THE WORKPLACE
Patterns of loyalty in a business context in South Korea vary from those in western countries.

Loyalty to People
In Korea, people are employed, transferred and promoted on the basis of who they know. For this reason, personal connections are usually more important than ability. The best way to move up is to be completely loyal to someone 'on the rise', because when he finally has the power to fill positions, he will look to those who have been loyal to him. He would generally choose a loyal person over a more competent but unknown person.

Koreans are not particularly loyal to business organisations. If a better opportunity comes up, transferring to another company is natural. If one has been particularly loyal to a higher-positioned person in one's own company, when he is transferred, he may very well try to open a position for his follower. It is a comfortable arrangement: he is happier having a loyal person working for him, and his follower sees it as his just reward for being faithful.

Loyalty to Companies

When you do major business with one business group in South Korea, you should do most of your smaller contracting through them, too. If you shop around to get the best price, you may be viewed as disloyal and your business dealings will suffer.

Even at the outset, if you approach several different companies about a particular proposal, you may find them all rejecting you. Your behaviour, in their opinion, has not been 'sincere'. Do not imagine your initial enquiries can be kept secret, because business people meet regularly to socialise and word may get out. It is best to do research about the various companies beforehand, and then concentrate on the one that appears most useful to you.

WORKPLACE ETIQUETTE

As a foreigner, you will not be expected to follow Korean etiquette to the letter. But there are a few differences you would do well to remember.

Respect

The person occupying the highest status in an organisation, such as company president or owner, deserves complete respect. His or her needs and desires traditionally come before any other aspect of the business. Employees are to be ready and willing to assist him or her at any time, in any way.

If you work for a Korean president, owner or principal, he or she probably will not expect you to follow the Korean rules of behaviour, but you should not forget that his or her position is higher than yours, and you are not equal in any sense.

REFRESHMENTS

Whenever you visit someone's office, you will be served something to drink. You will often not be asked beforehand what you would prefer, but it is impolite to refuse what you are offered. You will not always be asked which kind of drink you want or how you prefer your coffee or tea.

Likewise, when someone comes to your office, you should serve them something. It is not necessary to ask your guests what they want. Korean secretaries are accustomed to preparing coffee or fruit juice, but some more educated ones may not like serving drinks. If you have this situation, delegate the job to another person in the office; it would not be proper for you to make or serve refreshments.

Refreshments During Business Meetings

- Don't accept too eagerly; refuse the first offer
- Follow your host's lead
- It is considered impolite not to drink
- Sometimes you will not be given the selection of refreshments most westerners are used to

---

GIFTS

Gifts are a common way of showing appreciation, or getting someone to view you more favourably. They are sometimes given during important Korean holidays, such as the New Years, Lunar New year and Chusok. If you receive a gift at such times, it is important that you send a reciprocal gift. It is sometimes appropriate to bring a gift when visiting someone's office as well, particularly if you have been abroad recently.

BUSINESS ENTERTAINING

As in other countries, entertaining is an important part of doing business in Korea. The only difference is the degree to which entertaining seems necessary.

To begin a business relationship with someone, one generally dines and drinks. Then, to solidify the relationship, regular socialising is necessary. During negotiations, drinking and dining can soothe the way for easier discussions. And finally, after a business agreement has been made, regular social contact is advisable because when inevitable business kinks appear, there will be a relationship of friendship and trust to fall back on to solve problems amicably.

Do not overlook the role of alcohol. Drinking with someone is a sign of trust and drinking a lot with someone breaks down social barriers quickly. You may be surprised at how much easier business becomes, within and outside your own organisation, after a night of hard drinking. A person who drinks much may be viewed as more trustworthy.

Alot, perhaps even the majority, of business is conducted outside the office. To Koreans, the mood or the social atmosphere (the Korean *kibun*) is extremely important. Therefore, significant amounts of money are spent to create a conducive atmosphere. This always includes outstanding food, plenty of alcohol and sometimes beautiful women. Today, some younger Koreans are beginning to resist the expectations for heavy socialising and drinking.

When you are treated to one of these delightful evenings, it is important that you also invite your host to a similar event. Failing to reciprocate would show you to be greedy. This form of socialising is usually done in groups and includes several people from the businesses concerned. When people of equal status go out, they alternate who pays the whole bill which in turn enhances a sense of closeness and goodwill between colleagues.

PARTICULAR WORK SITUATIONS
Women in the Workplace
Like most countries, Korean women may not be treated as well in the workplace as their male counterparts in terms of salaries and promotions. Nevertheless, Korean women have made significant strides in the world of work over the last twenty years. Men and women work comfortably side by side and some companies even have policies to increase the number of professional women employees.

Expatriate women who work in Korea will be treated differently than foreign men but also with more respect than Korean women are generally shown. It is awkward for a Korean man to be supervised by a woman so the women will need to take care to establish her position of power while at the same time, treating her subordinates with kindness. Sexual harassment, including comments and inappropriate physical contact, may be experienced by western women working in Korean organisations, particularly in the context of drinking. Such behaviour violates Korean law and need not be tolerated. A simple and stern 'no' or 'stop that', is likely to end such behaviour. Women workers are not always invited to participate in the important after-work socialising but at the same time, it is easier for a woman to refuse these time-consuming events than it is for a man. Koreans recognise that women are responsible for caring for their families.

> ## First Paycheque
> Getting a new job is a significant event in anyone's life and Koreans mark this occasion by spending much of their first paycheque on their family and friends. Traditionally, new underwear was bought for all of one's family members, presumably because, at that time, underwear was a luxury. Now it is more common to give money to family members and treat friends to a meal.

Expatriate women working in Korea want to be mindful to dress conservatively. Clothes that might not be considered seductive in one's home country may reinforce the image Koreans have of western women being sexually free and may invite unwanted advances. Low-cut blouses or short skirts, though worn by young Korean women out having fun, are best avoided by western women when in the presence of work colleagues.

Supervising Korean Subordinates

Korean workers generally have more supervision and monitoring than their western counterparts. They are accustomed to receiving specific instructions, in other words, being micro-managed. It can be intimidating for them to work independently on project X which is to be completed by next week as they have been schooled to please their boss. Likewise, it can be difficult for Koreans to multi-task and manage their own time among several different projects. In the Korean workplace, they would be told what to work on and when so not being accustomed to making decisions by themselves, they are likely to be anxious that they won't make the choices their supervisor would want them to make.

Recognising that your expectations are unusual for them is the first step in helping them to work more independently.

Workplace Efficiency Standards

Many expatriates working in Korea discover two things: that Koreans spend an inordinate amount of time at work and that they do not accomplish as much as their western counterparts in the same amount of time. Because of this, expatriates may become frustrated, preferring that people use their work time better so that they could have more time at home or for relaxing but the Korean workplace is not organised around accomplishing tasks in the same way that western organisations are. Being at work and showing one's dedication is critical. If one is going to be at work for many hours, it is not always necessary to work at one's highest capacity. Likewise, as Korean workers are judged more on following the orders of their boss than on completing a particular group of tasks, they may not focus as much on finding the most efficient way to accomplish something. This is not to say that some Koreans don't work incredibly hard as some do and often for long hours.

ENGLISH TEACHERS IN KOREA

Confucian tradition confers a high status to teachers. Teachers and students may have life-long relationships; students are expected to show complete respect and teachers are expected to act with integrity, pass on their great wisdom and help students when asked. Korean students and their teachers know their roles and responsibilities well and when western teachers do not follow these norms, students become somewhat unclear about how to act.

Most students, from primary school students to business people attending language institutes, will show respect towards their western teacher. They are also likely to appreciate the relative informality that expatriates often bring to the classroom. Nevertheless, discarding all standards of respect would not be wise. Too much casualness may be confused with insincerity or lack of preparation. Korean students are accustomed to showing respect for their

A talented Korean man with a small business hand-crafting drums which are widely used in Korean folk festivals.

teachers and it works best for teachers to accept respect and behave in a manner that deserves this honour.

English teachers are viewed differently, depending on their employer. University teachers are most respected, followed by teachers in primary, secondary schools or colleges. Teachers at language institutes, while still valued, are not conferred as much respect. Some language institute teachers have placed a higher priority on having fun than on being a good teacher and thereby hurt the reputation of other institute teachers. In all settings, once students see that you are organised, knowledgeable and kind, they will appreciate your hard work and want to know you better. It is appropriate for English teachers to meet with adult students outside of class time, recognising that student-teacher roles remain, regardless of location. A popular website for English teachers (and others) in Korea is Dave's ESL Café; http://www.eslcafe.com/forums/korea/index.php.

Most people moving to Korea to teach English are able to save money and do some travelling during the teaching vacation. The place where one works impacts one's pay, schedule, working conditions and housing so it is essential to research the organisation you plan to work for prior to beginning employment. The number of hours and the general schedule should be specified, as some classes begin at 6:00 am and others end at 11:00 pm. Key questions to ask are: What is the vacation schedule and will the organisation pay for moving and travel expenses? Will medical insurance be provided? It is helpful to talk to former or current teachers to learn about their experience. How big are the classes? How well-behaved are the students? How satisfied were they with their housing? What is it like living in that particular city?

RECOGNISE THAT SOME THINGS IN THE WORKPLACE WILL REMAIN A MYSTERY

When asked why things at work are done a certain way, most expatriates have been told "It's the Korean way", as if that is enough of an explanation to the rational westerner. Westerners would be similarly hard-pressed to explain some of their work customs. Understanding how Korean organisations and businesses operate is beyond the comprehension of most expatriates and insisting on understanding will only result in exasperation. In other words, expatriates would do well to accept many things as uncomprehendable and move on with their work. One is not expected to do this in one's own culture, nor do Koreans do it in their work situation, but as a foreigner, it really is best to let some things go unexplained. To continue to seek a rational explanation will only result in frustration.

FAST FACTS
ABOUT KOREA

CHAPTER 10

'Even a sage follows the customs of his own time.'
—A Korean Proverb

Official Name
Republic of Korea

Capital
Seoul

Flag
White base with a yin-yang symbol (red on the top and blue at the bottom) in the middle. Near each corner of the flag is a different black trigram taken from the Book of I-Ching.

National Anthem
Aegukka

Time
Greenwich Mean Time plus 9 hours (GMT +0900)

Telephone Country Code
82

Land
Located at the southern half of the Korean Peninsula, the country is bounded in the north by North Korea. The Sea of Japan is found off its western coast and the Yellow Sea off its eastern coast. The Korean Strait to the south and southeast of the country separate it from Japan.

Area
total: 98,480 sq km (61,192.6 sq miles)
land: 98,190 sq km (61012.4 sq miles)
water: 290 sq km (180.2 sq miles)

Highest Point
Halla-san: 1950 m (6397.6 ft)

Major Rivers
Han River, Geum River and Nakdong River

Climate
Temperate climate with heavy rainfall in summer

Natural Resources
Coal, graphite, lead and tungsten

Population
48,598,175 (July 2004 est)

Ethnic Groups
Korean, with a very small number of Chinese

Religion
Buddhism, Christiantiy and Confucianism. About 46 per cent claim no affiliation to any religion while another one per cent practice in other religions.

Languages
Korean

Government
Republic

Administrative Divisions
Nine provinces called *do*:
Jeju (Cheju), Kangwon, Kyonggi, North Cholla (Cholla-bukto), North Ch'ungch'ong (Ch'ungch'ong-bukto), North Kyongsang

(Kyongsang-bukto), South Cholla (Cholla-namdo), South Ch'ungch'ong (Ch'ungch'ong-namdo) and South Kyongsang (Kyongsang-namdo)
Seven metropolitan cities called *gwangyoksi* :
Inchon, Kwangju, Pusan, Seoul, Taegu, Taejon and Ulsan

Currency
Korean won (KRW)

Gross Domestic Product (GDP)
US$ 857.8 billion (2003 est)

Agricultural Products
Barley, fruit, rice, root crops and vegetables

Other Products
Cattle, chickens, eggs, fish, milk and pigs

Industries
Automobile production, chemicals, electronics, shipbuilding, steel and telecommunications.

Exports
Computers, motor vehicles, petrochemicals, semiconductors, ships, steel and wireless telecommunications equipment

Imports
Electronics and electronic equipment, oil, organic chemicals, machinery, plastics, steel and transport equipment

Ports And Harbours
Chinhae, Inchon, Kunsan, Masan, Mokp'o, P'ohang, Pusan, Tonghae-hang, Ulsan, Yosu

Airports
Estimated at 102 of which 88 have paved runways

CULTURE QUIZ

Reading about Korean culture is one thing. Actually living in Korea is another. The purpose of this quiz is to help you imagine some of the situations that might confront you while you are living in Korea.

Ten of the most common difficulties that newcomers to Korea come across are described below. There are several alternative answers to choose from. A discussion follows about why some answers are better than others.

SITUATION 1

A Korean neighbour stops by your house to deliver your mail, which had inadvertently been left at her home. You begin a friendly conversation, during which you offer her some coffee. She politely refuses. What should you do?

A Take her answer at face value, and drop the subject?

B Bring her coffee anyway?

C A little later, ask her if she wants coffee again?

D Assume that she's Buddhist, and offer her tea as Buddhists don't drink coffee?

Comments

In Korea it is sometimes considered rude to accept something right away. So her refusal may well be out of politeness. When someone visits your home, it is always proper to serve your guest something, and serving something is probably more important than if the guest actually enjoys what you serve.

The best answer in this case would be **C**, but if she refuses again, bring her refreshment anyhow. Answer **B** would be second best. In fact, it is acceptable to bring something to your guest without consulting her first. Sometimes sugar and cream are added to coffee without consulting the guest.

Answer **A** would be considered rude, and answer **D** is simply not true.

SITUATION 2

You are out drinking with some Korean colleagues. Shortly after you arrive, the waitress brings glasses and a few bottles of beer. One colleague hands a glass to you. What do you do?

ⓐ Pass the glass on to the person next to you?

ⓑ Hold it while your colleague fills it, then hand him an empty glass to hold while you pour?

ⓒ Fill it and hand it back to the person who gave it to you?

ⓓ Consider it an honour, and fill it and all the other glasses with beer, one for each person present?

Comments

In social drinking, it is normal for a person to hand an empty glass to another person. The receiver should hold the glass as the giver pours the alcohol, as in answer **ⓑ**. Later, the receiver should pour alcohol for his drinking partner. Answers **ⓐ**, **ⓒ** and **ⓓ** will all be met with confused and embarrassed smiles.

SITUATION 3

You get on a crowded city bus. There is no place to sit, so you stand next to a seated woman. A few minutes later you feel the woman pulling at your package. What do you do?

ⓐ Hand her your package, since it is not worth much, and assume she is collecting for a charity.

ⓑ Scream in any language you know, to prevent her from stealing your money.

ⓒ Give her your package and smile.

Comments

It is common etiquette in Korea for seated passengers on buses to hold the packages of those standing. This is usually done nonverbally. Answer **ⓒ** is the best answer. Answer **ⓐ** would be all right, but you would be surprised when she gave it back to you as she got off the bus. Answer **ⓑ** would embarrass the woman as well as yourself.

SITUATION 4

You are at a party and start up a friendly conversation with a person you have met only a few times. One of the first questions he asks you is 'Why aren't you married?' You do not wish to answer. What do you do?

Ⓐ Explain that it is none of his business, and walk away as soon as possible?

Ⓑ Joke that there are no partners good enough for you?

Ⓒ Lie that you are married already?

Ⓓ Ignore the question and change the subject?

Comments

Personal questions are seen as a way to show one's concern for another. In no way does the person mean to be nosy. Answer **Ⓓ** would be the best answer. Answer **Ⓐ** would damage the other person's kibun. If the lie in answer **Ⓒ** were found out, you would not be viewed favourably. Answer **Ⓑ** may be viewed as a joke, but it may be seen as a lack of humbleness.

SITUATION 5

On your birthday, a former Korean student drops by your house with a small gift. What do you do?

Ⓐ Invite him in, thank him for the gift, and offer him something to drink.

Ⓑ Invite him in, open the gift in his presence, and ask him to stay for the next meal.

Ⓒ Tell him you appreciate the thought, but that you cannot accept such a gift. This is done to prevent the obligation of any favours.

Ⓓ Thank him for the gift and remember to find out his birthday so that you can send him a gift on that day.

Comments

Koreans consider the relationship between teacher and student to be lifelong. It is not unusual for a student to give his teacher a gift, even when the teacher is no longer teaching him.

Answer **A** is the best answer. Answer **B** is impolite because after the gift is opened the giver might be embarrassed at how small it is. Returning the gift, as in answer **C**, would be rude and unnecessary. Teachers have no obligations to a student because of a small gift. Nor is it appropriate for a teacher to give a birthday gift to a student, as in answer **D**. The teacher is obviously of higher status.

SITUATION 6

You are walking down the street with friend Mr A. He meets Mr B, whom you do not know. After a few minutes, you realise that you are being excluded from the conversation, and that you have not even been introduced. What do you do?

A Do not worry about it. Assume that Mr B is someone you do not need to know?

B Do not say anything, thinking that Mr A is indirectly insulting you?

C Introduce yourself to Mr B?

D Mention to Mr A that you have not been introduced to Mr B?

Comments

It is not usual for people who meet casually to introduce their companions. A chance meeting will probably last only a few minutes, after which each person will go his own way. Answer **A** is best. Answer **B** is totally incorrect. Answers **C** and would make everyone uncomfortable. Remember that if there is any reason for you to meet the other person, your friend would introduce you.

SITUATION 7

You are driving your car along a city street on a beautiful, seemingly peaceful afternoon. Suddenly, you hear a loud siren blaring on and off. Other cars pull over, and a man motions for you to do the same. What do you do?

Ⓐ Ignore the man and quickly make your way to your country's embassy?

Ⓑ Pull your car over to the side of the road. Lie down on the floor of your car?

Ⓒ Pull your car over and sneak into a nearby coffee shop for 20 minutes?

Comments

If you remember the date, this is probably happening on or around the 15th of the month. It is the monthly civil defence drill. The siren can scare the newly arrived expatriate. People must get off the road, but remaining in one's car is acceptable. It is best to take shelter in a nearby building, making **Ⓒ** the best answer.

If you proceeded to head towards your embassy, as in answer **Ⓐ**, you would meet strong resistance. Lying down, as in answer **Ⓑ**, is unnecessary.

SITUATION 8

It is the middle of January and you are trying to figure out some way of lowering your enormous heating bill without dying of pneumonia. Your maid comes to work and the first thing she does is to open all the windows and begin cleaning. What do you do?

Ⓐ Assume she thinks your apartment is too hot, and question her sanity?

Ⓑ Realise that she is indirectly asking to be fired, and kindly let her go?

Ⓒ Explain to her that you never want the windows open in the winter?

Comments

Koreans tend to like their homes warmer than their Western counterparts. But they feel that fresh air, every day, is very important. They also believe that when one is cleaning, the windows must be open so that the dust can get out. (Apparently, Korean dust never enters through the window!).

Most homes in Korea are heated by the ondol system of hot water pipes beneath the floor. Traditionally, the walls of the home did not keep heat in very well, so the best way to keep warm was to sit on the warm floor. Sitting there, open doors or windows were not a problem.

Answer **C** is the only appropriate answer, but you may need to make an effort to enforce such a policy. In the summer, wire mesh anti-insect screens are thought to keep in the dust while cleaning. So, before cleaning, your maid will probably open all the screens.

SITUATION 9

You have heard about an end-of-year office party for a few days, but have received no formal invitation. One day, a colleague informs you that the boss will be hosting the party at his house. What do you do?

A Ask your colleague when the party begins, and go?

B Assume that since you were not invited by the boss, you had better not go. Naturally, you feel hurt?

C Assume that the boss has your best interests at heart, and did not invite you because you would feel uncomfortable at the party?

D Casually ask the boss if he knows anything about the party?

Comments

Invitations in Korea are almost always informal, and often not made by the person hosting the event. Other people in your office probably know when the party is, and your colleague made a special point of telling you, since you may not have understood the Korean chatter about the party. Answer **A** is clearly best.

Since you are part of the office, any party given for the office would include you. Your being foreign is irrelevant. Answers **B** and **C** are incorrect for that reason.

There is nothing wrong with asking the boss, as in answer **D**, but it is really unnecessary. And he may worry that he had inadvertently hurt your feelings by not clearly inviting you.

SITUATION 10

You are enjoying a drink after a lovely dinner with a group of your closest Korean friends, who are of the same sex as yourself. Much to your dismay, you realise that the hand of one friend is resting on your thigh. What do you do?

Ⓐ After realising that this 'friendship' has a different meaning for your friend, you make an excuse and escape quickly?

Ⓑ Realising that this is one way of showing friendship in Korea, you reciprocate by resting your hand on your friend's thigh?

Ⓒ Feeling uncomfortable, you quietly say that in your home country, people do not do this?

Ⓓ Accept his touch without reciprocating?

Comments

In Korea, physical expression between people of the same sex is natural and comfortable. There is no homosexual connotation to such-behaviour. Answer **Ⓐ** would be totally incorrect. If you feel comfortable, answer **Ⓑ** would be a good answer, or answer **Ⓓ**. If not, it is best to let your friend know, as in answer **Ⓒ**.

DO'S AND DON'TS

DO'S
General

- Show affection as a sign of friendship between people of the same sex.
- Remember that Koreans express their affection for children through touching them. Once used to it, children enjoy the attention given to them.
- Remember you are expected to bargain in markets. After asking the price, give the seller a counter-offer. Finally, agree on a price somewhere between the seller's offer and your own. Bargaining is not done at supermarkets, department stores or other places where the price of merchandise is already marked.
- Bow when greeting another person for the first time. If the discrepancy in status is very great, only the person of lower status bows, while the other responds verbally. When two people are introduced, they also bow.
- Treat the elderly with kindness and respect at all times. Bus and underground train seats should always be offered to them. If an elderly person has trouble crossing the street, or trouble carrying something, a younger person is obliged to help.
- Preserve social harmony as much as possible; you may have to tell small lies, or adopt indirect, less efficient behaviour than in the west.
- Remember that status is important. It is determined primarily by profession, family and age. Acknowledging other people's status will make social relationships smoother. It is also necessary to act according to one's own status. For example, a maid's status is lower than that of their employer and they are most comfortable working when that distinction is clear.
- Do address Koreans, by their title, for example, Manager Kim, President Lee, Assistant Director Park. This shows respect and helps to identify the innumerable

Mr Kims, Mr Lees and Miss Parks. If you can learn to say the titles in Korean, a closer feeling will then be established.

- Pass objects to someone of equal or higher status with the right hand. To show the most respect, two hands are used, or the right hand supported by the left. When passing objects to people of lower status, either hand is acceptable, but using two hands is not appropriate.
- Remember that highly educated people are respected, and what they say is listened to carefully.
- Remove all footwear before entering someone's home, or when entering a temple. In offices and other public places, shoes are not removed.

Work

- Greet and bow the first time you see each person each day.
- Get a third party formally to introduce you to a potential business associate. Self-introductions are rarely successful in Korea.
- Always carry business cards, preferably printed in English and Korean, and make sure that you give one to acquaintances during the introduction.
- Establish a good relationship before you discuss any work. Develop social networks, both among expatriates and Koreans, to help you in future work transactions.
- Remember that in Korean society, smooth social relationships often take precedence over organisational or business efficiency.
- Recognise that entertaining is an essential part of doing business, and that the cost of entertaining may far exceed what it costs in your home country.
- Be flexible. Pushing too hard will certainly not be viewed favourably.
- Remember that 'yes' does not always mean 'yes'.

Dining And Entertainment

- Remember that invitations are generally given informally. They are usually verbal, and not always given by the person hosting the event. Invitations are rarely given more than a few days in advance, and sometimes only a few hours before the event.

- Prepare gifts. Fruit, flowers, cakes or alcohol should be given whenever visiting someone's home. On special occasions, such as a first birthday, a gift is also appropriate. When one attends a wedding, a 61st birthday party or a funeral, money in an envelope is appropriate.

- Prepare more food for guests than would be necessary by western standards. Generosity towards friends and acquaintances is important. This includes giving gifts that are worth a bit more than one might expect. Being at all stingy is impolite.

- Remember that drinking is an important part of social and business relationships for men in Korea. The amount of alcohol consumed at any given time is generally considerably more than most westerners are accustomed to consuming.

- Be prepared to sing a song or two at any social gathering. At parties, the most honoured person is given the first chance to sing. Other people are then each given a turn.

- Remember that eating is done with chopsticks and a large spoon. Rice is served on the left, and soup on the right. The person of highest status should begin the meal. Excessive talking during the meal is considered impolite. Slurping is acceptable, as a sign of enjoyment.

- Remember to eat your *kimchee* cautiously at first as it is usually quite spicy. *Kimchee* is the national food made from pickled Chinese or *napa* cabbage. Koreans will be very pleased to see you enjoy your *kimchee*.

- Remember that paying is considered an honour and also a matter of pride. Paying is done by the person who did the inviting. 'Going Dutch' is never done. If there is a question as to who made the invitation, the bill is fought over.

DON'TS
General
- Show affection between the sexes in public.
- Show your anger. It is impolite, and can permanently damage interpersonal relationships. Keep your temper at all times.
- Criticise. When absolutely necessary, it must be done tactfully, gently and privately.
- Dress too informally. The way you dress reflects your position. Also, it is a sign of respect, so when meeting people, or when visiting someone's home, one should dress nicely and conservatively. Shorts, backless dresses, and so on are not appropriate in public.
- Expose money unless you are paying at the market or at a shop. When giving a gift or when paying an employee, money should be put in an envelope.
- Be impatient when services are not performed on time, someone is late, or things are not done efficiently.
- Answer personal questions if you do not wish to answer them. Simply change the subject. These questions may include 'Why aren't you married?' and 'How old are you?' and are simply a way Koreans use to get to know another person.
- Write people's name in red. In Korea, it is only done when people have died.

Work
- Assume that everyone in Korea understands your language. Get into the habit of having people paraphrase what you say, and do not be afraid to write down key points.
- Cause anyone to lose face. Always allow an 'escape'.
- Use the telephone for business communication. Use face to face contact.
- Criticise anything Korean.

Dining And Entertainment
- Wear shoes when entering a Korean home.
- Waste rice. Rice is the staple of the Korean diet. Throwing away leftover rice is considered wasteful and bad luck.

- Tip before checking if a service charge has already been added to the bill. This is done in some first-class hotels. However, if the service at a restaurant, hairdresser or in a taxi has been especially good, a small tip would be appreciated.
- Don't accept a Koreans offer to pay for dinner when you have done the inviting. It is natural for them to offer but you should insist on paying.

GLOSSARY

USEFUL WORDS AND PHRASES
Greetings and Common Courtesy

How do you do?	*Cho-um peop-gessoyo? (informal)*
Good morning/ afternoon/ evening or How are you?	*Annyong haseyo (used any time of day)*
Thank you	*Kamsa-hamnida*
I am sorry	*Mee-an hamnida*
I am glad to see/meet you	*Mannaso pan-gawoyo*
Come in	*Tul-o oseyo*
Good bye	*Annyong he gaseyo*
Yes, there is/we have	*Ye, issoyo*

Transportation

Will you show/tell me the way to the Seoul City Hall?	*Seoul shi-chong kanun kilul karucho chuseyo?*
Where is the ballpoint pen?	*Ballpoint pen e odi issumnika?*
Where can I get a taxi?	*Odeso taxi-rul talsoo itsul kayo?*
Over there	*Cho-ke yo.*
How long does it take to Seoul railway station?	*Seoul-yeok kkaji olmana kollim- ni ka?*
It takes about 15 minutes	*Yak ship-o-boon kollimnida*
Please stop here/ over there	*Yogi/chogi so sewo chuseyo*
How far is it to Kwanghwamoon?	*Kwanghwamoon ggaji olmana momneka?*
Does this bus go to Kangnam?	*Yee bus-ka Kangnam kamneka?*

Shopping

Please show me this wristwatch	*E-shegye rul poyo chooseyo*
How much is it?	*E-geot-eun olma imnika?*
I would like to buy this	*E-geot-ul sa-ke-sumnida.*
Please wait for a moment	*Chom-shi keedalyo cheseyo*

Eating Out

May I have a menu, please?	*Menu chom chuseyo*
What is your speciality here?	*Chal-hanun umsik-e mu-eot ip-nika?*
What would you recommend?	*Muosi mashi-isumnika?*
Give me the same as his/hers	*Katun kosuro cheseyo.*
Don't make it too spicy	*Nomu maep-chi-anke hae-chuseyo*
Give me one-portion (two-, three-)	*Il-in-boon (e-in-boon, sam-in-boon) chuseyo*
It is delicious	*Mashi-soyo.*
Please give me a glass of water	*Mool chooseyo*
Please give me some more of this	*E-geot teo chuseyo*
I enjoyed the meal	*Chal mogosumnida*
Cheque, please	*Kyesanso chuseyo*
How much is it?	*Olma imnika?*
It is W5,000/ 10,000/ 15,000/ 20,000/ 30,000.	*O-chon/maan/maan*
Can I pay it with my credit card?	*Kredit kaduro kyesan halsu isumnika?*

FREQUENTLY USED WORDS

Bank	*Eunhaeng*
Hospital	*Pyong-won*
Police station	*Kyochalso*
Post office	*Woo-chae-gook*
School	*Hakkyo*
Toilet	*Hwajangshil*
Address	*Chooso*
Automobile	*Jadongcha*
Bicycle	*Jajungo*
Book	*Chaek*
Breakfast	*Achim shiksa*
Currency/check	*Hyngeum/soo-pyo*
Dinner	*Joyok-shiksa*
Funeral	*Changrye shik*
House	*Jib*
Lunch	*Jomshim*
Men's/ women's clothing	*Namja/yeoja ot*
Money	*Ton*
Name	*Erum, songmyong*
Shoes	*Shin, kootoo*
Sleeping	*Jam*
Socks	*Yangmal*
Stamp	*Woo-pyo*
Wedding	*Kyol hon*
Spring/ summer/ autumn/ winter	*Pom/ yeorum/ ka-eul/ kyo-eul*
Hot/cold/warm (temperature)	*Ttu-keo-un/cha-ga-un/ ttatteut-han*
East/west/south/north	*Tong/seo/nam/book*
Hot/ salty/ sweet/ bitter	*Maep-ssumnida/ tchamnida/ shinggop-sumnida/ ssumnida*

Brother/ sister	*Hyongje/ nooe*
Father/ mother	*Aboji/ omoni*
Grandfather/ grandmother	*Haraboji/ halmoni*
Grandparents	*Chobumo*
Grandson/ granddaughter	*Sonja/ sonnyo*
Policeman/ policewoman	*Kyongchal*
Professor/ teacher	*Kyo-shoo/ sunsaeng*

COMMONLY USED ENGLISH WORDS

Virtually everyone uses and/or understands these words:

- ballpoint pen
- baseball
- bell
- bicycle
- bowling
- car
- coffee/coffee shop
- college
- cooking
- dancing
- golf
- goodbye
- ink
- milk
- money
- sex
- soccer
- tea
- tea room
- tennis
- university

RESOURCE GUIDE

If one is calling from Seoul one need not dial the (02) prefix; however, if one is using a mobile phone one must dial the (02) prefix, even when in Seoul. These websites and phone numbers may change.

IMPORTANT TELEPHONE NUMBERS (NO PREFIX NEEDED ANYWHERE IN THE COUNTRY)

- Police   **112**
- Fire, Emergency or Ambulance   **119**
- 24 Hour Medical Referral Service for foreigners
  010-4769-8212 or 010-8750-8212

USEFUL PHONE NUMBERS AND WEBSITES

- Directory Assistance   **114**
- International Call and Information   **0074**
- International Operator   **0077**
- International access code   **001**
- Seoul Help Center For Foreigners
  Tel: (02) 731-6800
  Website: http://shc.seoul.go.kr
- Life In Korea
  Website: http://www.lifeinkorea.com/
- Korean National Tourism Organisation:
  Website: http://english.tour2korea.com
  Tel: (02) 729-9600, or also dial 1330 anywhere in Korea.
- The Korean Overseas Information Service
  Website: http://www.korea.net
- Seoul Metropolitan Gov't
  Tel: (02) 3707-8768
  Website: http://english.seoul.go.kr
- Invest Korea
  Website: http://www.kisc.org
- Help Service Korea
  Tel: (02) 720-0870 (housekeeping, childcare)
  Website: http://www.hnskorea.com

- Hanaro Telecom
  Website: http://www.hanaro.com/eng/
- Korea Thrunet Co.
  Website: http://english.thrunet.com/service/multi_cable.asp
- Onse Telecom Co.
  Website: http://www.onse.net/eng/index.asp

Telecommunications Providers

- SK Telink 00700 (Discounted International Calls)
  Tel: (02) 3709-1115
  Website: http://www.sktelink.com
- Dacom Telecity 002
  Tel: (02) 1544-4663
  Website: http://foreign.telecity.co.kr
- SK Telecom
  Tel: (02) 6343-9011
  Website: http://www.sktelink.com/english/index.html
- LG Telecom
  Tel: (02) 1544-0010
  Website: http://www.lgtelecom.com/eng/index.jsp
- Korea Telecom Corp
  Tel: (02) 1588-0010
  Website: http://www.kt.co.kr/kthome/eng/prod/pro_info/prod_ps.jsp

Post Office

http://www.koreapost.go.kr/

Transportation

- Korea Travel Phone
  Dial 1330 from any phone in Korea for English speaking travel assistance.
- Korea mass transit info portal
  Website: http://www.odsay.com/en/site.asp
- Seoul Underground Train Map
  Website: http://www.subwayworld.co.kr/english/index.htm
- Seoul Bus Maps
  Website: http://english.seoul.go.kr

- Seoul Station & Cheongnyangni Station
  Tel: (02) 1544-7788 (ext 2)
- Express Bus Lines Association:
  Tel: (02) 1588-6900
  Website: http://www.kobus.co.kr/eng/index.jsp
- Korea National Railroad
  Tel: (02) 1544-7788
  Website: http://www.korail.go.kr/ROOT/main-top.
  top?lang = eng
- Ferries
  http://english.seoul.go.kr/residents/transport/trans_11fer.html

Banking

- Industrial Bank of Korea
  Tel: (02) 729-7068
  Website: http://www.kiupbank.co.kr
- Kookmin Bank:
  Tel: (02) 1588-9999 ext. 30
  Website: http://www.kbstar.com
- Korean Exchange Bank
  Tel: (02) 729-8406
  Website: http://www.keb.co.kr/english/
- Shinhan Bank
  Website: http://www.shinhan.com

Medical

In Seoul, a 24-hour English speaking emergency medical referral service can be reached at 010-4769-8212 or 010-8750-8212. Less urgent referrals can be emailed to medicalreferral@seoul.go.kr.

Western Clinics/Hospitals

- Hurest Wellbeing Club
  Tel: (02) 778-7700
  Website: http://www.hurest.co.kr
- Samsung Medical Center:
  Tel: (02) 3410-00200
  Website: http://english.samsunghospital.com

- Asan Medical Centre
  Tel: (02) 3010-5001/(02)3010-3333 (emergency)
  Website: http://www.amc.seoul.kr/ ~ int
- Seoul National University Hospital
  Tel: (02) 760-2890/011-9150-2890 (emergency)
  Website: http://www.snuh.snu.ac.kr
- SNUH Foreigner's clinic
  Website: http://snuh.snu.ac.kr/hosp/ic/index_ic.html
- Severance Hospital, Yonsei University
  Tel: (02) 361-6540/ (02) 392-3404
  012-263-6556 (emergency)
  Website: http://www.severance.or.kr/en
- Korea University Medical Center
  Tel: (02) 920-5894
  Website: http://www.kumc.or.kr/all/english/index.jsp
- Soonchunhyang University Hospital
  Website: http://www.schuh.ac.kr/exam/center_info.
  asp?idx = 15
  For emergency call (02) 709-9158/ 011-321-9161

Oriental Medicine

- Dong-So Oriental Hospital
  Tel: (02) 337-1110/ (02) 332-0001 (emergency)
  Website: http://www.dsoh.co.kr
- Gangnam IN Oriental Medical Clinic: (foreign medical doctor)
  Tel: (02) 547-8575
  Website: http://www.inisgood.com
- Hospital of Jaseng Oriental Medicine
  Tel: (02) 3218-2000
  Website: http://www.jaseng.net

Dental Clinic

- Kim Min Hee International Dental Clinic
  Tel: (02) 3472-7528/ (02) 3473-7528
- Ye Dental Clinic
  Tel: (02) 556-1393/ (02) 555-4375 (emergency)
  Website: http://www.kangnam.yedental.com

Real Estate and Relocation Services

- Crown Relocation
  Tel: (02) 796-5717
  Website: http://www.crownrelo.com
- Dreamland Realty
  Tel: (02) 794-0811
  Website: http://www.relocationkorea.net
- Eden Realty (Noksapyeong/Itaewon)
  Tel: 017-685-8565
  Website: http://www.edenrealty.co.kr
- Happy Housing
  Tel: (02) 790-9770
  Website: http://www.happyhousing.co.kr
- Korea Real Estate Info Centre
  Tel: (02) 539-5423
  Website: http://www.kreic.com
- Korea Relocation Service
  Tel: (02) 790-7967
  Website: http://www.relocation.co.kr
- Lucky Realty
  Tel: (02) 792-8277
  Website: http://www.luckyrealty.net
- N.D. Consulting
  Tel: (02) 795-7968/ 017-254-5099
  Website: http://www.ndconsulting.co.kr
- Reloko
  Tel: (02) 558-0021
  Website: http://www.reloko.com
- Solomon
  Tel: (02) 793-6699
  Website: http://www.solomonirc.com

Schools for Expatriate Children

- Busan International School
  Tel:(051) 747-7199
  Website: http://www.busanforeignschool.org
- Centennial Christian School
  Tel: (02) 905-9275
  Website: http://www.ccslions.com/

- Chinese Primary, Middle and High School
  Tel: (02) 324-0664
- Early Childhood Learning Center (Montessori School)
  Tel: (02) 795-8418.
- Deutsche Schule Seoul
  Tel (02) 792-0797
  Website: http://www.dsseoul.org
- Ecole Internationale Xavier
  Tel: (02) 741-7688
  Website: http://www.xavier.sc.kr
- Seoul Academy International School
  Tel: (02) 554-0451
- Franciscan School
  Website: http://www.franciscanschool.com/
  Tel: (02) 798-2195
- Global Christian School
  Tel: (02) 797-0401
  Website: http://www.gcskorea.com
- International Christian School
  Tel: (02) 773-1993
  Website: http://icseoul.org
- Japanese School
  Tel (02)574-0348
- Korea International School
  Tel: (02) 561-0509
  Website: http://www.kis.orkkr
- Korea Kent Foreign School
  Tel: (02) 2201-7091-2
  Website: http://www.kkfs.org
- Seoul Foreign British School
  Tel: (02) 330-3100
  Website: http://www.sfs.or.kr/page.php?id = 2
- Seoul Foreign School
  Tel: (02) 330-3100
  Website: http://www.sfs.or.kr
- Seoul International School
  Tel (02) 2233-44551
  Website: http://www.sis-korea.org

Korean Language Schools

- Ewha University
  Tel: (02) 312-0067
  Website: http://elc.ewha.ac.kr
- Korean Language Education Culture Center
  Tel: (02) 511-9314
  Website: http://www.edukorean.com
- Sogang University
  Tel: (02) 705-8088
  Website: http://sgedu.sogang.ac.kr/korean/
- Yonsei University
  Tel: (02) 2123-3464–65
  Website: http://165.132.13.12/~kli/

Religious Services

Buddhist

- International Buddhist Information Center
  Website: http://www.buddhapia.com/eng
- Jogyesa Temple
  Tel: (02) 732-2115
  Website: http://www.ijogyesa.net
- Lotus Lantern Int'l Buddhist Center
  Tel: (02) 735-5347
  Website: http://www.lotuslantern.net
- Templestay
  Tel: (02) 732-9925 ~ 7
  Website: http://www.templestaykorea.net

Catholic

- Catholic Church in Korea English
  Website http://www.cbck.or.kr/eng/en_index.htm
- Myeondong Cathedral
  Tel: (02) 774-3890 (ext. 0)
  Website: http://www.mdsd.or.kr
- Yeoksam Catholic Church
  Tel: (02) 553-0801 (ext. 0)
  Website: http://www.englishmass.com

Protestant
- Church of Christ (Osan, Youngsan, and Kunsan)
  Website: http://eng.christ.or.kr/
- Church of Jesus Christ of Latter- Day Saints
  Tel: (02) 2232-3637
- Seoul Union Church: www.seoulunionchurch.org
  Tel: (02) 333-7393/ 011-9773-9076
- Youngnak Presbyterian Church
  Tel: (02) 2280-0228/ 011-613-5896
  Website: http://iwe.youngnak.net
- SaRang Community Church
  Tel: (02) 3479-7706
  Website: http://english.sarang.org
- The Anglican Church of Korea
  Tel: (02) 738-6597
  Website: http://www.seouldiocese.net
- International Lutheran Church
  Tel: (02) 794-6274
  Website: http://www.ilcseoul.net/
- Seventh Day Adventist
  Website: http://www.cs.hongik.ac.kr/ ~ swkim/sahch.html
- Yeouido Full Gospel Church
  Tel: (02) 782-4851
  Website:http://yfgc.fgtv.com
- Yongsan Baptist Church
  Tel: (02) 796-0284/ 011-731-0573
  Website: www.yongsanbaptist.org

Islamic
- Korea Muslim Federation
  Tel: (02) 793-6908
  Website: http://www.koreaislam.org

Korean Traditional Music and Dance Performances
- Chindo Regional Culture Centre
  Tel 0632-544-3710

- Chongdong Theater
  Tel: (02) 7511-500
  Website: http://www.chongdong.com/english/main.htm
- National Centre for Korean Performing Arts
  Tel: (02) 580-3054
  Website: http://www.ncktpa.go.kr/index_eng.html
- Pusan Cultural Centre
  Tel 051-623-0179
- Sejong Cultural Centre
  Tel: (02) 399-1111
  Website: http://www.sejongpac.or.kr/index.asp

Communities and Clubs

- Alcoholics Anonymous in Korea
  Tel: (02) 319-5861
  Website: http://www.aainkorea.org/
- Cross-Cultural Awareness Group (CCAP)
  Tel: (02) 755-4623 ~ 5
  Website: http://ccap.unesco.or.kr
- International Spouses of Koreans Association (ISKA)
  Tel: 016-891-2991
  Website: http://www.iskakorea.com
- Seoul Club
  Tel: (02) 2238-7666
  Website: http://www.seoulclub.org
- USO (United Service Organisation)
  Tel: (02) 795-3028
  Website: http://www.uso.org/korea
- Irish Association of Korea
  Website: http://www.seoulshamrock.co.kr
- Seoul Foreign Correspondent's club
  Website: http://www.sfcc.or.kr

Women's Communities

Seoul International Women's Association (http://www.siwapage.com) has current information about other organisations for women in Korea.

- American Women's Club (AWC)
  Tel: (02) 744-7752
  Website: http://www.awckorea.org
- Australia & New Zealand Association (ANZA)
  Website: http://www.anzakorea.org or
  anzaseoul01@yahoo.com
- British Association of Seoul (BASS)
  Email: basseoul@yahoo.co.uk
- Canadian Women's Club (CWC)
  Tel: 011-9087-7278
- Dutch Club
  Tel: (02) 744-6751/ 019-498-0705
  Website: http://www.hamelinkorea.com
- German Club
  Tel: (02) 793-6671/ (02) 790-2466
  Website: http://www.deutscherclubseoul.com
- Irish Association of Korea
  Website: http://www.seoulshamrock.co.kr
- Korean Association of University Women (KAUW)
  Tel: (02) 993-2378
  Website: http://www.kauw.or.kr
- Nordic Women's Club (NWC)
  Tel: (02) 793-9229
- Swedish Women's Educational Association (SWEA)
  Tel: (02) 794-6441
  Website: http://www.chapters-swea.org/seoul
- Working Women's Network
  Email: siwawwnseoul@yahoo.com

Bookshops

- Seoul Selection
  Tel: (02) 734-9564–65/ (02)734-9565
  Website: http://www.seoulselection.com
- Kyobo Book Centre
  Tel: (02) 3704-2000
  Website: http://www.kyobobook.co.kr
- What The Book
  Tel: (02) 797-2342
  Website: http://www.whatthebook.com

Useful websites about living in or visiting Korea

- http://english.seoul.go.kr/
  The Seoul City Hall website for foreigners living in Seoul.
- http://www.kexpat.com/
  A website for expatriates in Korea
- http://www.Koreainfogate.com
  News, movie reviews, transportation and yellow pages for foreigners living in Korea.
- http://www.lifeinkorea.com/index.cfm?Language = English
  A website which focuses on services for foreigners in Korea.
- http://tour2korea.com/
  An attractive website created by Korea National Tourism Organsation with a special focus on travel in Korea.
- www.Visitseoul.net
  A website with updated information about Seoul life.
- http://www.worldexecutive.com/cityguides/seoul/
  A website geared to business people working or living in Korea.

FURTHER READING

LIVING IN KOREA

Culture Smart! Korea. James Hoare. Portland, Oregon, USA: Graphic Arts Publishing, 2005

- A helpful, brief introduction to Korean customs and etiquette. The book addresses the culture in both North and South Korea.

Faces of Korea. Richard Harris. Seoul: Hollym, 2004.

- The author interviewed 47 people from 20 countries about their varied experiences living in Korea. Together, they give one a deeper understanding of the commonalities and differences in foreigners' lives in Korea.

Focus on Living in Seoul. American Chamber of Commerce in Korea, 2003. Available through the Seoul Help Centre for Foreigners. Email: hotline@scoul.go.kr

- This book gives comprehensive, updated information about everything, from planning your move to Korea to shopping in Korea and what to do and see. Many indispensable phone numbers are included.

Living in South Korea. Rob Whyte, Kyong-Mi Kim. Vermont, USA: Pro Lingua Associates, 2004.

- This book is a concise introduction to living in South Korea, written by two people who taught English in Busan.

KOREAN CULTURE

The Art of Crossing Cultures. Craig Storti. Yarmouth, ME, USA: Intercultural Press Inc., 1990.

- This book explains the phenomenon of culture shock in depth and gives practical advice on how to make the adjustment. It does not specifically address Korean culture but is useful to expatriates living in Korea.

Crosscurrents. Susan Pares. Seoul: Seoul International Publishing House, 1985.

- This is a collection of articles originally written for The Korean Herald. The author is an expatriate who writes about some of the joys and sorrows of living in Korea. Though now dated, it still illuminates important aspects of Korean culture for expatriates.

Communication Styles in Two Different Cultures: Korean and American. Myung Seok Park, Seoul: Han Shin Publishing Co., 1979.

- This book gives some theoretical background to intercultural communication, and then highlights some of the difficulties of communication between Koreans and Americans. Some of the examples are quite entertaining

A Guide to Korean Cultural Heritage. The Korean Overseas Culture and Information Services. Seoul: Hollym, 1998.

- This book provides in-depth details about traditional Korean cultural practices.

Korea: An Introduction. James Hoare and Susan Pares. London: Kegan Paul International Limited, 1988.

- A comprehensive introduction to many aspects of Korea, including politics and history, culture, social structure and the spiritual side.

Korean Cultural Potpourri. Kyu-tae Jeon. Seoul: Seoul International Publishing House, 1987.

- This book is a series of articles, originally published in the English-language newspaper, The Korean Herald. They are interesting and well-written, explaining Korean culture from a Korean's perspective.

Korean Patterns. Paul Crane. Seoul: Kwangjin Publishing Co., 1978.

- This book was first published in 1967, by a medical missionary to Korea. It is a classic in understanding the way Koreans think and act. Since it was written over 20 years ago, it describes an earlier Korea, but many of the customs are still practised.

Land of Morning Calm: Korean Culture Then and Now. John Stickler and Soma Han Stickler. Fremont, CA, USA: Shen's Books, 2003.

Looking at Each Other. Marion E. Current and Dong-ho Choi. Seoul: Seoul International Publishing House, 1983.
- Humorous illustrations and short descriptions contrast Korean culture with western cultures.

Proverbs, East and West. Compiled by Kim Young-chol. Seoul: Hollym, 1991.
- An anthology of Chinese, Korean and Japanese sayings, which provide a delightful window into understanding these different ways of thinking.

Through a Rain Spattered Window. Michael Daniels. Seoul: Taewon Publishing Company, 1973.
- The author of this book lived in Korea for 15 years. The book is a collection of insightful essays on topics such as the family, time and weather and Confucian tradition.

KOREAN HISTORY
Korea's Place in the Sun: A Modern History. Bruce Cumings. London: W W Norton & Company, 1997.
- An in-depth, academic examination of recent Korean history by a scholar who has devoted his life to this topic.

The Two Koreas: A Contemporary History. Don Oberdorfer. New York, USA: Basic Books, 2002.

Women of Korea. Ed. Yung Chung Kim. Seoul: Ewha Woman's University Press, 1976.
- This is an introduction to the history of Korea from ancient times to 1945, paying particular attention to Korean women. The details about individuals' lives make it fascinating to read.

KOREAN BUSINESS

Korean Business Etiquette: The Cultural Values And Attitudes That Make Up The Korean Business Personality. Boye Lafayette De Mente. Tuttle Publishing, 2004.

- For the business person, this book covers everything from the personal nature of business to Korean unions and advertising barriers.

The Koreans: Who They Are, What They Want, Where Their Future Lies. Michael Breen. New York, USA: St Martin's Press, 1999.

NTC's Dictionary of Korea's Business and Cultural Code Words. Boye Lafayette De Mente, Singapore: McGraw Hill, 1998.

KOREAN COOKING

Growing Up in a Korean Kitchen: A Cookbook. Hi Sooshin Hepinstall. Berkeley, CA, USA: Ten Speed Press, 2001.

Korean Home Cooking (Essential Asian Kitchen Series). Soon Yung Chung. Tuttle Publishing, 2001.

- A clearly written, beautifully photographed, and highly rated cookbook.

The Korean Kitchen: Classic Recipes from the Land of the Morning Calm. Copeland Marks. San Francisco CA, USA: Chronicle Books, 1999.

Traditional Korean Cuisine. Woul Young Chu. Los Angeles: Jai Min Chang. The Korea Times, L.A., 1985

- A nicely illustrated cookbook, with clear, easy-to-follow recipes. There is a section on table settings and table manners.

TOURISM IN KOREA

Insight Guides: Korea. Hong Kong: Apa Productions (Hong Kong) Ltd., 2003.

- This book provides sensitive, in-depth information on a variety of Korean topics with a focus on travel in South

Korea. The photographs are reason enough to buy this guide.

Lonely Planet Korea. Martin Robinson, Andrew Bender, Rob Whyte, John Banagan. London: Lonely Planet Publications, 2004

Moon Handbooks South Korea. Robert Nilsen. Emeryville CA, USA: Avalon Travel Publishing, 2004.

KOREAN LANGUAGE

College Korea. Michael C Rogers, Clare You and Kyungnyun K Richards. California, USA: University of California Press, 1992.

Elementary Korean (Tuttle Language Library). Ross King, Jae-Hoon Yeon. Tuttle Publishing, 2004.

KOREAN ADOPTION

Beyond Good Intentions: A Mother Reflects on Raising Internationally Adopted Children. Cheri Register. St Paul MN, USA: Yeong & Yeong Book Company, 2005.
- Written by a woman who has adopted two Koreans daughters who are now adults.

The Unforgotten War: Dust of the Streets. Thomas Park Clement. Bloomfield IN, USA:Truepeny Publishing Company, 1998.
- One of the few autobiographies written by a male Korean adoptee, this author describes his life from a loving Korean home, to the streets of Seoul, to an adoptive family and his road to becoming a successful business person.

I Wish for You a Beautiful Life: Letters from the Korean Birth Mothers of Ae Ran Won to Their Children. Trans. Sara Dorow. St Paul MN, USA: Yeong & Yeong Book Company, 1999
- Poignant letters written by Korean women whose children have been adopted.

A Single Square Picture: A Korean Adoptee's Search for Her Roots. Katy Robinson. New York, USA: Berkley Publishing Group, 2002.
- A heart-wrenching account of her life as a Korean adoptee.

The Language of Blood: A Memoir. Jane Jeong Trenka. St Paul MN, USA: Borealis Books, 2003.
- A young woman describes her life as a Korean-adoptee in rural America and her reunification with her family in Korea.

Ten Thousand Sorrows: The Extraordinary Journey of a Korean War Orphan. Elizabeth Kim. New York, USA: Doubleday, 2000.
- An emotional story of one woman's journey as a Korean adoptee to the United States.

KOREAN AMERICANS

East to America: Korean American Life Stories. Elaine H Kim, Eui-Young Yu. New York, USA: New Press, 1997.
- Fifty interviews with a variety of Korean-Americans, written by two Korean Americans.

Korean-Americans: Past, Present, and Future. Ed. Ilpyong J Kim. Seoul: Hollym International Corporation, 2004.
- A collection of articles compiled to commemorate one hundred years of Koreans in the United States.

To Swim Across the World. Ginger Park and Frances Park. New York, USA: Miramax Books, 2001
- A love story describing the author's experiences growing up in two different parts of Korea, meeting and coming to the United States.

One Thousand Chestnut Trees. Mira Stout. New York, USA: Riverhead, 1998.
- Authored by a Korean American, this novel roughly parallel's her own life, trying to learn about her motherland, Korea.

Quiet Odyssey: A Pioneer Korean Woman in America. Mary Paik Lee. Washington, USA: University of Washington Press, 1990.

- A powerful autobiography of one women's journey from Korea to the United States.

Still Life With Rice. Helie Lee. New York, USA: Scribner, 1997.

- The author travels from California to Korea to reconstruct the life of her grandmother in this beautifully written biography.

Translations of Beauty: A Novel, Mia Yun. New York, USA: Atria, 2004.

- A novel portraying the experience of a young Korean immigrant to the United States, making sense of her new country and her Korean parents' expectations.

RAISING CHILDREN ABROAD

Notes from a *Traveling Childhood: Readings for Internationally Mobile Parents & Children.* Ed. Karen C McCluskey. Washington DC, USA: Foreign Service Youth Foundation, 1994.

The Third Culture Kid Experience: Growing Up Among Worlds. David C Pollock and Ruth E Van Reken. Yarmouth ME, USA: Intercultural Press, 1999.

Third Culture Kids. David C Pollock. Boston MA, USA: Nicholas Brealey Publishing, 2001.

- This book identifies many issues that are important to children who are growing up abroad (and their parents).

Unrooted Childhoods : Memoirs of Growing Up Global. Faith Eidse. Boston MA, USA: Nicholas Brealey Publishing, 2004

ABOUT THE AUTHORS

Dr Vegdahl was born in the state of Minnesota, USA. She received her Masters in Social Work at the University of Chicago in 1981, shortly before moving to Korea, where she lived for seven years. She obtained her PhD in Social Work and Social Research at Portland State University and currently is a professor of Social Work at Concordia University in Portland, Oregon. Dr Vegdahl also does consulting for businesses that work with Korea and has a clinical practice working with individuals and families.

Born in Korea, Dr Hur came to the United States to obtain his MS in Speech Communication at Illinois State University and a Masters in Public Health at the University of California at Berkeley. He obtained his PhD in Higher Education/Speech Communication at the University of Iowa. He returned to Korea to teach for most of the 1980's. He currently teaches Speech Communication at Sierra College in Sacramento, California. Dr Hur also does research, writing and consultation in intercultural communication and health behaviours.

INDEX

Titles in the CULTURE**SHOCK**! series:

Argentina	Hong Kong	Paris
Australia	Hungary	Philippines
Austria	India	Portugal
Bahrain	Indonesia	San Francisco
Barcelona	Iran	Saudi Arabia
Beijing	Ireland	Scotland
Belgium	Israel	Sri Lanka
Bolivia	Italy	Shanghai
Borneo	Jakarta	Singapore
Brazil	Japan	South Africa
Britain	Korea	Spain
Cambodia	Laos	Sweden
Canada	London	Switzerland
Chicago	Malaysia	Syria
Chile	Mauritius	Taiwan
China	Mexico	Thailand
Costa Rica	Morocco	Tokyo
Cuba	Moscow	Turkey
Czech Republic	Munich	Ukraine
Denmark	Myanmar	United Arab
Ecuador	Nepal	Emirates
Egypt	Netherlands	USA
Finland	New York	Vancouver
France	New Zealand	Venezuela
Germany	Norway	Vietnam
Greece	Pakistan	

For more information about any of these titles, please contact any of our Marshall Cavendish offices around the world (listed on page ii) or visit our website at:

www.marshallcavendish.com/genref